THE MILITARY AND VETERAN 52-WEEK DEVOTIONAL

FIVE MINUTES OF DAILY INSPIRATION FOR WARRIORS OF FAITH

LIEUTENANT COLONEL CURT W. KOLVET

Five Vines Press

The Military and Veteran 52-Week Devotional
Five Minutes of Daily Spiritual Inspiration for Warriors of Faith

First Edition: January 2026
Printed in the United States America Publisher: Five Vines Press
For permissions or bulk orders, contact: cwkolvet@curtwkolvet.com

ISBN (Print): 979-8-9944027-0-2
ISBN (eBook): 979-8-9944027-1-9

Cover by Chuck Schotborgh www.sumochuck.com

Visit curtwkolvet.com for news, updates, and additional resources.

10 9 8 7 6 5 4 3 2 1

Thank You

My sincerest thanks to my family, friends, and all those that worked on putting this book together to reach those it was intended to help and share God's word with.

A profound thank you to all who have served, especially to the great and amazing patriots I had the pleasure of serving with or alongside for over 20 years, who inspired me throughout my career and still do to this day.

Most importantly thank you God for all of your blessings, for our savior Jesus Christ, and for making all things possible; one of which is this devotional, that I pray is solely for Your glory.

† TABLE OF CONTENTS

FOREWORD xi
PREFACE xiii
HOW TO USE xv

WEEK 1	*Joshua 1:9 (ESV)*	Courage 1
WEEK 2	*John 15:12 (ESV)*	Sacrificial Love 6
WEEK 3	*Psalm 56:11 (ESV)*	Trust Over Fear 11
WEEK 4	*Isaiah 53:5 (ESV)*	Healing Through Christ 16
WEEK 5	*Proverbs 3:5-6 (ESV)*	Trust And Direction 21
WEEK 6	*Romans 12:2 (ESV)*	Transformation 26
WEEK 7	*Philippians 4:6-7 (ESV)*	Peace Beyond Understanding 32
WEEK 8	*2 Timothy 1:7 (ESV)*	Power, Love, and Self-Control 37
WEEK 9	*Matthew 11:28-30 (ESV)*	Rest for the Weary 42
WEEK 10	*James 1:2-4 (ESV)*	Endurance Through Trials 47
WEEK 11	*Psalm 34:18 (ESV)*	God is Near the Broken-Hearted 53
WEEK 12	*Isaiah 40:31 (ESV)*	Strength to Endure 58
WEEK 13	*John 16:33 (ESV)*	Peace in the Middle of Trouble 64
WEEK 14	*Galatians 6:9 (ESV)*	Stamina in Doing Good... 70
WEEK 15	*Psalm 91:1-2 (ESV)*	Refuge and Fortress 75
WEEK 16	1 *Peter 5:7 (ESV)*	Casting Your Cares on God 81

WEEK 17	*Matthew 6:19-21 (ESV)*	Treasure in Heaven........86
WEEK 18	*Hebrews 12:1-2 (ESV)*	Endurance and Focus on Christ.............91
WEEK 19	*Romans 12:21 (ESV)*	Overcoming Evil with Good.....................96
WEEK 20	*Matthew 5:9 (ESV)*	Peacemakers 101
WEEK 21	*Proverbs 27:17 (ESV)*	Sharpening One Another 106
WEEK 22	*Ecclesiastes 3:1 (ESV)*	Seasons and Timing 111
WEEK 23	*2 Corinthians 5:17 (ESV)*	Created Anew............. 116
WEEK 24	*Psalm 23:4 (ESV)*	God's Presence............ 121
WEEK 25	*1 John 1:9 (ESV)*	Confession and Forgiveness 126
WEEK 26	*Jeremiah 29:11 (ESV)*	God's Plans and Hope.... 131
WEEK 27	*Ephesians 6:11 (ESV)*	Spiritual Armor 136
WEEK 28	*Romans 8:1 (ESV)*	No Condemnation 141
WEEK 29	*2 Timothy 2:3 (ESV)*	Enduring Hardship...... 146
WEEK 30	*Psalm 46:1 (ESV)*	God is Our Refuge...... 151
WEEK 31	*Colossians 3:23 (ESV)*	Work for the Lord........ 156
WEEK 32	*James 1:5 (ESV)*	Wisdom for Life's Decisions..................... 161
WEEK 33	*1 Peter 5:10 (ESV)*	Restoration After Suffering...................... 166
WEEK 34	*Job 11:16-19 (ESV)*	Hope After Hardship.... 171
WEEK 35	*Isaiah 41:9-13 (ESV)*	God Holds Your Hand.... 176
WEEK 36	*John 3:16 (ESV)*	The Ultimate Sacrifice.... 182
WEEK 37	*Romans 8:38-39(ESV)*	Unshakable Love 188
WEEK 38	*Matthew 6:25-27 (ESV)*	Freedom From Anxiety 194
WEEK 39	*Corinthians 12:7-10 (ESV)*	Strength in Weakness ..200
WEEK 40	*Proverbs 16:18-20 (ESV)*	Humility and Wisdom......................205
WEEK 41	*Philippians 4:12-13 (ESV)*	Strength in Every Circumstance 211
WEEK 42	*Psalm 41:1-2 (ESV)*	Compassion & Divine Protection 217

WEEK 43	*Matthew 5:2-12 (ESV)*	The Beatitudes............223
WEEK 44	*James 4:6-8 (ESV)*	Grace for the Humble...229
WEEK 45	*Luke 6:41-42 (ESV)*	Self-Examination Before Correction..................235
WEEK 46	*John 4:13-14 (ESV)*	Living Water................240
WEEK 47	*1 Timothy 6:10-12 (ESV)*	Fight the Good Fight...246
WEEK 48	*Romans 15:13 (ESV)*	Abounding in Hope..... 251
WEEK 49	*Hebrews 13:15-16 (ESV)*	Praising and Worship...256
WEEK 50	*John 14:1-6 (ESV)*	The Way, The Truth, and The Life 262
WEEK 51	*Mark 12:28-34 (ESV)*	Greatest Commandment............267
WEEK 52	*John 3:5-7 (ESV)*	Born Again..................272

ABOUT THE AUTHOR 277
BIBLIOGRAPHY...281

FOREWORD

Over the years I have seen many Service members serving in the military step into faith with fear, joy and celebration! Without question military service can profoundly shape a person's relationship with God. In moments of uncertainty, fear, and sacrifice, many service members come to rely more deeply on their faith, discovering strength they didn't know they had, strength that comes from leaning fully on God. In many of these situations finding God for the first time! Military life, especially when we are deployed, often strips away distractions and reveals what truly matters, helping individuals see that their highest calling isn't just to serve their country, but to walk faithfully in the purpose God has for their life. Service time is limited; for each of us a time came when it was time to take off the uniform and move to the next season of our lives when our time of military service came to an end.

BUT, lasting service, rather an eternity of service, is the calling that God places on those who call Jesus their Savior. Men and women who are committed to God, grounded in His truth, and led by His Spirit. To stay strong in that commitment, we must make it a daily habit to spend time in God's Word, allowing it to shape our hearts, renew our minds, and deepen our connection with Him. Through trials, discipline, and the demand for courage, faith becomes more than belief it becomes a lifeline. Curt has put together a great devotional that will guide you in growing in your faith and strengthen your commitment to SERVING the commander of the universe, our Lord and Savior Jesus Christ.

Proverbs 3:5–6 (NIV)

"Trust in the Lord with all your heart and lean not on your own understanding; in all your ways submit to him, and he will make your paths straight."

- **Chaplain (Lieutenant Colonel) Todd V. Brown, U.S. Army**

PREFACE

To all your life's questions, there is one answer; to all your problems there is one solution, and that is Christ.

There is only one instruction on how to use this devotional, and that is to approach it with an open heart, mind, and soul, listening for what God is trying to tell you. After that, use this tool to help you strengthen your faith, build your relationship with God, and improve your spiritual life as you wish; so that you, a warrior for Christ, may be victorious in this time of spiritual warfare you're confronted with every day. If you're opening this up and reading, you're already winning!

Many devotionals I have read in the past have been great, however, often every day is: a different message, a different passage, a completely different context without transitions or themes. Therefore, I developed this devotional to be a week-long study on one verse each week, to help not only learn the passage of scripture but to really spend the time to reflect and meditate on it properly. I also labeled each week with a theme so that you can pick the week that most applies to you and the season in life you find yourself. This devotional was written to take no more than 5 minutes a day (more if you wish) to review a singular verse or passage each day for a week; study it, reflect on it, apply critical thinking, and see examples of how to live out that scripture in your own life.

It is important for me to state that the words and the teachings and principles in this devotional are not my own, they are God's and the results of our Savior coming to this earth and sacrificing Himself for us, so that we are promised a new birth, a new life, and eternity in His name. I simply put them into a format I believe was inspired to be written in a way to be helpful to those like me, who served. I take no credit, all credit truly goes to God, and I pray sincerely and genuinely this devotional helps you; is deserving of His name; and will serve for His Glory.

After over 20 years of service in the Army working alongside the sister services overseas, in garrison, and even domestically, I found myself at the end of a privileged and blessed career. My body aching daily, my life on the home-front changing, and a desire to move on to a new chapter of life, were all calling me to transition. I assessed myself and I knew something had to change, I had to be better, I had to be ready, and I couldn't just continue on how I always had. How do I go forward, in what way, in what manner, were the questions that continually would come to the forefront of my mind.

I'm embarrassed now that I even had to ask those questions, the answer was so obvious and was always there. You go forward in Christ! Though having always been a Christian, I recognized I wasn't where I needed to be in my faith and I needed to reconnect spiritually, become a student of the Gospels, and have a more sincere, focused, robust relationship with Christ and reside in His love as I face these new big moments in my life. Writing this devotional has helped me immensely with doing a better job of walking with Christ daily in my life; I pray if you're anything like me, transitioning out of service, or still in, that you will be rewarded by reading this devotional in the same ways I have been in writing it. May God bless you and guide you on your journey, and remember, have no fear for God is with you wherever you go!

HOW TO USE

Day 1: The Beginning: Becoming familiar with the Week's Key Verse.

Days 1-6: Deeper Dive: Read the Key Verse each day then read the Mission Insights for further understanding of the verse and its lessons. Do the Personal Inspection question, meditate on your answer, and when you are ready say the ending prayer for the day.

WEEK 33 † RESTORATION AFTER SUFFERING

Key Verse: *1 Peter 5:10 (ESV)*

"And after you have suffered a little while, the God of all grace, who has called you to his eternal glory in Christ, will himself restore, confirm, strengthen, and establish you."

Day 1

Mission Insight
A follow on to Week 16, Peter wrote this to believers under persecution, people who knew pain and uncertainty. His words resonate for both service members and civilians who have also walked through suffering, both seen and unseen. This verse does not deny hardship it advocates resiliency through it. "After you have suffered" acknowledges the reality of pain, but the promise is stronger and more eternal than the pain; God will "restore, confirm, strengthen, and establish you". The suffering will not last but God's grace will, He is the One who heals, steadies, and rebuilds what the world has torn down.

Personal Inspection
Have you asked "Why me", "Why now", have you then said after "where to now God, lead the way"?

Prayer
God, I do not always understand the suffering I am walking through, but I trust that You are not finished! Restore and strengthen me today so that I may continue marching on for Your Glory.

Day 2

Mission Insight
The phrase "a little while" can feel insulting when you've been suffering for a while. But Peter isn't minimizing your pain He is magnifying eternity. All who have endured long stretches of adversity can find hope here, your current struggle is not the end of your story, not even close, keep the faith.

Personal Inspection
What hardship feels endless right now and how might this verse give you eternal perspective?

Prayer
Lord, help me lift my eyes beyond today's pain. Anchor me in the hope of what You are still doing and will do.

Day 7: The Review: Re-read the Key Verse then read the After Action Reflection of our week on the verse. See the auxiliary references that supports our week's message to look up if you wish. Then say a prayer to close out the week. Additionally, there is a "Field Note" added for you to see an example or testimonial that helps illustrate the verse from the week.

Day 7 - After-Action Reflection

This week reminded us that suffering is real but so is God's restoration. You have not been abandoned. You have been *called*. You have not been ruined you are ready to be restored. We need to acknowledge going forward; no pain is wasted, and no journey is too off course for God to rebuild us or redirect us. He will strengthen what is weak, steady what is shaken, and confirm what's eternal. This is grace and it is personal to you.

Auxiliary Scriptures
- *Romans 5:3–5* "Suffering produces endurance… and hope does not put us to shame."
- *Isaiah 61:3* "To give them beauty for ashes…"

Prayer
God of all grace, thank You that I am not forgotten. Restore what has been lost or broken, confirm what is true, and build my life on the foundation of Your goodness.

Field Note
Major Richard "Dick" Winters, commander of Easy Company, 506th PIR, 101st Airborne, during WWII (may sound familiar and if like me, you're a fan of "Band of Brothers"), endured brutal combat in Normandy, Operation Market Garden, and the Battle of the Bulge. After the war, Winters lived a quiet life, never seeking glory but seeking normalcy and peace. Despite a statue erected in his honor at Normandy, he remained humble and denied being a hero, but said he served with heroes. His post-war life exemplified restoration, strength from suffering and stability after chaos. ("MAJ Richard D. Winters," n.d.) As 1 Peter 5:10 promises, God had not just seen Winters through battle, He established him in grace and legacy far beyond war.

WEEK 1 † COURAGE

Key Verse: *Joshua 1:9 (ESV)*

> **"Have I not commanded you? Be strong and courageous. Do not be frightened, and do not be dismayed, for the Lord your God is with you wherever you go."**

Day 1

Mission Insight

This verse is God's charge to Joshua as he stepped into daunting, unfamiliar territory leading warriors into promised ground still occupied by enemies. It speaks powerfully to veterans and service members who understand what it is to stand on thresholds where danger and uncertainty lie ahead. Here God roots Joshua's courage not in his own preparation or strength, but in the unbreakable promise of God's presence. This calls each of us to ground our courage in knowing God goes with us, no matter the terrain.

Personal Inspection

Where are you facing fear right now, and what would it look like to ground your courage in God's presence rather than your own strength?

Prayer
Lord, help me absorb this command deep in my heart. Teach me to draw courage not from my experience alone, but from the assurance that You are truly with me wherever I go.

Day 2

Mission Insight
Deployment orders, new assignments, or even starting new lives or careers can stir anxiety, like stepping into unfamiliar missions with no guarantees. This verse reminds us that courage isn't the absence of fear but moving forward in the conviction that God travels with us. His command to be strong flows directly out of His promise to never leave us alone.

Personal Inspection
Where are you stepping into something unknown right now, and how could God's promise reshape your approach?

Prayer
God, steady my heart as I walk into what I can't control. Anchor my courage in Your faithful presence.

Day 3

Mission Insight
Memories of combat or the weight of old fears can follow those who have served long after the battlefield. God's words to Joshua cut through lingering dread with a call to rise-up, knowing fear doesn't get the final say. His presence becomes the firm ground where we can stand unafraid.

Personal Inspection

What old fears might you need to lay at God's feet to embrace His courage today?

Prayer

Jesus, You see the hidden shadows I still carry. Fill me with Your strength where I feel weak.

Day 4

Mission Insight

Families of service members have experience with constant uncertainty, enduring countless goodbyes and waiting seasons. God's charge to be courageous stretches beyond warriors to those who keep the home fires burning, promising that wherever we go or they are, near or far, He is there too.

Personal Inspection

How might God's presence change the way you handle the long separations or silent battles left in the wake of service at home?

Prayer

Lord, watch over those I love while we're apart or moving forward in a new life together. Help us all rest in knowing You are with us wherever we are and anywhere the path leads.

Day 5

Mission Insight

Transitioning out of military service or engaging back into civilian life can feel like stepping onto foreign ground. God's words to Joshua echo here, reminding us that strength and courage for new roles and uncertain futures come from knowing we never walk alone.

Personal Inspection
What part of your future feels most intimidating right now, and how does God's promise meet that fear?

Prayer
Father, calm my anxious thoughts about what's next. Lead me forward with confidence grounded in Your faithful guidance.

Day 6

Mission Insight
Hours of training build readiness, yet even seasoned warriors can face moments of doubt. This verse speaks into those vulnerable spaces, assuring us that the truest source of courage isn't our preparation, it's God's unshakable companionship.

Personal Inspection
How could trusting God's promise to be with you make you bolder in facing life's next test?

Prayer
God, deepen my trust beyond what I've rehearsed or prepared for. Make Your presence the strongest part of my courage.

Day 7 After-Action Reflection

This week we explored how true courage is built not on our grit or experience, but on God's unchanging nearness. Whether stepping into new seasons in our lives, carrying memories of old battles, navigating long separations, or taking leaps of faith, His command remains: be strong and courageous for He is with you. As we carry this verse forward, may it anchor every unknown, and redefine what brave looks like.

Auxiliary Scriptures

- *Deuteronomy 31:6* "Be strong and courageous. Do not fear or be in dread of them, for it is the Lord your God who goes with you."
- *Psalm 27:1* "The Lord is my light and my salvation; whom shall I fear? The Lord is the stronghold of my life; of whom shall I be afraid?

Prayer

Lord, thank You for speaking courage into my life this week. Help me stand strong in every challenge, not by my own might, but because You go before me. Teach me to trust Your presence more deeply with every step I take.

Field Note

On D-Day during WWII, soldiers stormed the beaches of Normandy under relentless enemy fire, advancing not because danger suddenly disappeared, but because the mission and the path ahead to victory demanded it. Their courage rose out of conviction that holding back was not an option. Joshua 1:9 mirrors this kind of forward-leaning faith; it calls us to move even when afraid, because God Himself goes with us. For those who have served, this promise should give us renewed courage in every step we take, proving real strength is found in trusting the One who never abandons the fight.

WEEK 2 † SACRIFICIAL LOVE

Key Verse: *John 15:12 (ESV)*

"This is my commandment, that you love one another as I have loved you. Greater love has no one than this, that someone lay down his life for his friends."

Day 1

Mission Insight

Jesus spoke these words on the night of His betrayal, just before laying down His life. His definition of love is not sentimental, it is sacrificial. This verse is etched into the hearts of warriors who have seen, and sometimes participated in, acts of selfless bravery. In the military, "laying down your life" might happen in an instant, but it also happens in quiet, daily sacrifices be it long deployments, missed moments, enduring danger for the sake of others. Jesus doesn't just admire this kind of love; He commands it. He set the ultimate example living out his own words by having given His life for us.

Personal Inspection

What does sacrificial love mean to you, and do you embody this type of love as Jesus exemplified?

Prayer
Lord Jesus, thank You for showing us the truest form of love. Help me live out that love, not only in dramatic moments, but in the ordinary sacrifices You ask of me every day.

Day 2

Mission Insight
Service demands sacrifice, some obvious, some invisible. The love Jesus describes isn't just for combat or crisis, it's a lifestyle. Whether it's giving up your time, comfort, or control; sacrificial love means placing someone else's well-being ahead of your own. It's easy to love in theory, harder in practice.

Personal Inspection
Where in your life are you being called to love sacrificially even when it's inconvenient?

Prayer
Lord, help me love others in ways that cost me something. Teach me to see sacrifice not as loss, but as obedience and gaining more that I am losing.

Day 3

Mission Insight
Love can leave scars as most people know, and we understand that sacrificing for others may lead to grief, pain, or long-term burdens. But Christ's love shows us that wounds borne for others are not wasted. He redeems them. His scars became the very sign of victory and healing, and He invites us to see our sacrifices through that same lens.

Personal Inspection

What scars emotional or physical remind you of the love you have given?

Prayer

God, heal the places in me marked by love given at great cost. Show me how You're using even those wounds for good and give me the confidence to keep loving as you have.

Day 4

Mission Insight

Some sacrifices aren't dramatic, they're daily choices to lay down ego, control, or convenience. It might mean letting someone else lead, choosing not to retaliate in an argument, or staying present for someone who's struggling. These acts of love often go unnoticed, but they don't go unnoticed by God.

Personal Inspection

What small sacrifice could you make today that would show someone they matter?

Prayer

Jesus, teach me to love in the quiet, humble ways You modeled. Make me alert to the needs around me.

Day 5

Mission Insight

Transitions throughout military service can feel like losing that clear sense of purpose or identity especially with retirements or change of duty locations as examples. But this verse reminds us that the mission to love doesn't end with retirement or a permanent change of station. Civilians, active duty, and veterans alike are called to keep loving, to keep laying down comfort for the good of others, in family, church, community, our past colleges or friends, and beyond.

Personal Inspection
Where do you feel God calling you to bring the same mission-minded love you practiced in service?

Prayer
Lord, show me where my next assignment of love lies. Give me eyes to see that my purpose in You never ends.

Day 6

Mission Insight
Fear can hold us back from loving well. Fear of rejection, failure or getting hurt can hold us back from loving well. But Jesus' love pushed through fear, even unto death. The kind of love He calls us to isn't reckless, but it is brave, to show up in love even when it's hard.

Personal Inspection
What fear is standing between you and deeper love, by Jesus' example can you be emboldened?

Prayer
Jesus, give me courage to love through the fear. Help me trust that You'll meet me on the other side of obedience to Your example.

Day 7 After-Action Reflection

Jesus doesn't suggest sacrificial love, He commands it. This week we've seen that true love costs something, but it never comes back empty. Whether on the battlefield, in the home, or at the side of someone in need, laying down your life for others mirrors Christ's own mission. You may not be called to die for a friend but you are called to live for others. That's where Christ-like love shines brightest.

Auxiliary Scriptures

- *Philippians 2:3–8* "Have this mind among yourselves, which is yours in Christ Jesus..."
- *Romans 5:8* "But God shows His love for us in that while we were still sinners, Christ died for us."

Prayer

Jesus, thank You for laying down Your life for me. Help me reflect that same love in how I speak, act, and serve. Make me someone who doesn't just admire sacrificial love but lives it.

Field Note

Desmond Doss, an Army medic during World War II, with the 77th Infantry Division, served in the Pacific theater without ever carrying a weapon due to his religious beliefs. He was ridiculed for his values, yet during the Battle of Okinawa, he saved the lives of 75 men by dragging them one by one to safety under heavy fire, though he himself being severely wounded twice. Doss' courage and selflessness earned him the Medal of Honor, yet his actions were rooted in conviction of faith and love for his fellow man, not medals. (Congressional Medal, 2025) He was willing to lay down his life over and over again, without needing a weapon to do it. His life embodied John 15:13 in action. Real love risks everything for others.

WEEK 3 † TRUST OVER FEAR

Key Verse: *Psalm 56:11 (ESV)*

**"In God I trust; I shall not be afraid.
What can man do to me?"**

Day 1

Mission Insight
David wrote this psalm while under enemy surveillance and capture, facing real threats, real danger. But his response was not panic or hopelessness; it was trust. Those that know the uniform, know that courage isn't the absence of fear but the decision to act anyway. In the military, fear is managed by training and preparation but even then, some moments call for deeper strength. David shows us where that strength is found, in God. When you know who holds your life, the power of fear is broken. This verse isn't bravado; its quiet confident faith forged under pressure.

Personal Inspection
What does it mean to trust God, do you truly trust God's strength to address/face your fears?

Prayer

God, help me trust You more than I fear what's around me. Teach me to stand steady, not because I am strong, but because You are.

Day 2

Mission Insight

Fear is often loud and persistent. Trust doesn't have to shout and be loud, it simply holds firm. For those of us who have returned home, we may no longer face enemies with weapons, but instead we face fear of failure, rejection, or not measuring up. David's words offer a steadying truth; no threat has more power than God's promise, and in God you can have victory over fear and its many forms.

Personal Inspection

What's the loudest fear in your mind right now, and how can trust in God quiet it?

Prayer

Lord, help me choose trust even when fear feels more familiar. Remind me You're still in control.

Day 3

Mission Insight

Many that served carry private fears, memories that haunt, decisions that linger, relationships that feel fragile, or failures of the past we keep present in our current day. But David shows us the pathway forward, speak trust aloud. Not to deny the fear or what this world tries to do to us, but to declare that God is bigger than it all! Saying "In God I trust" isn't weakness; it's warfare against fear and the past, ensuring our promised future.

Personal Inspection

What fear needs to be named and surrendered to God today?

Prayer

Jesus, I give You the fears I've carried in silence. Replace them with Your peace and strength knowing you have prepared a place for me this world can never take away.

Day 4

Mission Insight

Trust is often tested in life's many transitions. Whether it's retirement from the military, a new job, or a move across the country, any uncertainty can rattle us. David's verse reminds us that God is constant, even when we find that we and our lives are not. The world may shift but our foundation doesn't, and is how we can stay surefooted in life's ever-changing seas.

Personal Inspection

What recent change has shaken your sense of security and stability?

Prayer

Father, be my anchor in this season of life that I am in today. Help me trust You more than my circumstances and know that these seasons in life are temporary and you are eternal.

Day 5

Mission Insight

Fear thrives on worst-case scenarios. It magnifies what might go wrong. But David asks a bold rhetorical question, "What can man do to me?" It's not that people can't hurt us, it's that they can't define us, they cannot remove us from Him. When our identity is rooted in the God who protects, redeems, and restores we are untouchable in spirit.

Personal Inspection

Who or what have you given too much power in your thoughts that doesn't deserve it, and how can you take it back through trust and place it in its proper perspective?

Prayer

God, help me reclaim peace where I've let fear take over. You are my Defender.

Day 6

Mission Insight

Trusting God doesn't mean nothing bad will ever happen. It means nothing can ultimately destroy you when you revere Him. That's the promise David clung to and it's the one we inherit through Christ. God's love makes us resilient, and through Him all things are possible.

Personal Inspection

What fear are you ready to replace with the certainty of God's love, are you prepared to be bold knowing that through God's love you will be ok?

Prayer

Jesus, nothing can separate me from Your love, may I always be thankful to You for this and help me live boldly in this Truth!

Day 7 After-Action Reflection

This week reminded us that fear is real, but it's not the boss. David faced literal enemies and still declared, "In God I trust." For military and civilians alike, that trust isn't about blind optimism it's about confidence in the One who never changes. Whatever battle you face, external or internal, trust can be your weapon. Speak it, live it, and let it shape your steps.

Auxiliary Scriptures

- *Isaiah 41:10* "Fear not, for I am with you..."
- *Romans 8:31* "If God is for us, who can be against us?"

Prayer

God, anchor my heart in Your promises. Teach me to trust You when fear rises and to walk boldly knowing You go before me.

Field Note

Colonel Joshua Lawrence Chamberlain, commander of the 20th Maine Infantry Regiment during the Civil War, is best known for his pivotal role in defending Little Round Top during the Battle of Gettysburg in July 1863. A former theology college professor Chamberlain volunteered to fight believing the war was a moral struggle over the soul of the nation. At Gettysburg, outnumbered and nearly out of ammunition, Chamberlain ordered a daring bayonet charge that repelled Confederate forces. Throughout the war, Chamberlain frequently demonstrated personal courage under fire, wounded six times in the war, he once wrote, "I fear only to fail in doing my duty, nothing else." (White, 2024) His life echoes the spirit of Psalm 56:11: "In God I trust; I shall not be afraid. What can man do to me?" Chamberlain's trust in God's sovereignty gave him the strength to face death without flinching and to lead with honor.

WEEK 4 † HEALING THROUGH CHRIST

Key Verse: *Isaiah 53:5 (ESV)*

"But he was wounded for our transgressions; he was crushed for our iniquities; upon him was the chastisement that brought us peace, and with his stripes we are healed."

Day 1

Mission Insight

This verse, spoken by the prophet Isaiah centuries before the crucifixion, describes the suffering of the Messiah in visionary detail. It connects Christ's wounds directly to our healing. This is a profound reminder that pain whether physical, emotional, or spiritual, is not unfamiliar to God. The healing that Jesus offers isn't just theoretical or just in the future, it's personal, present, and available now! Through His wounds, our injuries can find restoration. Whether we carry scars on our body or in our hearts, Christ meets us in them, without shame and with redemption; as exemplified in His resurrection still displaying His own scars from the crucifixion.

Personal Inspection

Do you accept that Christ's wounds were for your salvation, that like He conquered his wounds, so too can you overcome yours through Him?

Prayer
Jesus, thank You for taking my pain upon Yourself. Help me trust that Your suffering wasn't wasted but deliverance and redemption is for me as well.

Day 2

Mission Insight
Some wounds are visible; others stay buried deep beneath the surface. Many of us often carry both. Isaiah 53:5 is an invitation to bring those injuries, whatever they look like, into the light of Christ's love. His stripes and wounds weren't just endured; they were purposeful; not only did they forgive our sins but His blood also brought a victory and peace where chaos once lived.

Personal Inspection
What wound have you kept hidden (He knows already) that Christ is ready to heal if you let Him?

Prayer
Lord, I open up the places I've kept closed. Let Your healing reach even there no matter how deep.

Day 3

Mission Insight
There's often a lie that we have to get better or be put together and not be a soup sandwich before coming to God. But this verse turns that on its head, Jesus was "crushed" because we are broken. He didn't wait for us to be whole. He came for us in the middle of the mess, and it's His wounds and sacrifice, not our efforts, that brought healing and salvation.

Personal Inspection
Where have you been trying to heal yourself without letting God in?

Prayer
Jesus, I surrender the part of me that's still trying to do it all alone. Be my Healer, bring me peace.

Day 4

Mission Insight
Families of warriors often bear invisible wounds too: anxiety, secondary trauma, emotional distance, this verse extends to them as well. Christ's healing is not limited to the one who served but also reaches to those who've walked beside, waited at home, or picked up the pieces. The warrior often gets the glory of service while the families also sacrificed in their own ways.

Personal Inspection
To serve is to serve at home too, how can you invite Christ's healing into your family's story?

Prayer
Lord, bless the ones who stood by me. Heal what's been strained or broken in our relationships, not only heal these relationships, make them better and stronger than before.

Day 5

Mission Insight
Some wounds heal, but the scars remain, and that's okay. Even the resurrected Jesus still bore His scars. They were not signs of defeat, but proof of love and victory over death, they became part of His

identity that even the disciple Thomas could not doubt. For veterans, scars, emotional or physical, can become testimony to God's power to redeem no matter what marks this world leaves on us.

Personal Inspection

What scar in your life might become a source of strength for someone else, how is God meaning to use you as a powerful example to reach others?

Prayer

Jesus, use even my scars for Your glory. Let them tell a story of healing, not defeat, of victory, not loss; like Jesus' victory over crucifixion and death so too will my scars lead me to Him.

Day 6

Mission Insight

Sometimes we carry guilt for things we've done or didn't do. This verse speaks directly to that burden. Christ was wounded for our transgressions, crushed for our iniquities. That means the price has already been paid. Forgiveness isn't something we earn it's something we receive through His grace and grace alone.

Personal Inspection

Is there a mistake or sin you're still carrying that Christ already paid for? He's ready to remove the load from your shoulders, to His. Are you ready to lighten your burden?

Prayer

God, thank You that my forgiveness doesn't depend on how I must earn it or pay for it, it's already been paid forward. You know my heart, help me know that Your grace is enough.

Day 7 After-Action Reflection

This week, we sat with the reality of wounds, both Christ's and our own. All of us living understand injury and the longing to be whole again, for many of us pain is a daily thing. Isaiah 53:5 reminds us that true healing comes not through forgetting the past, but through surrendering it to Jesus. His suffering brings us peace. His scars bring us strength. His death brings us life. You are not too broken for Him and you are not beyond healing.

Auxiliary Scriptures

- *1 Peter 2:24* "By His wounds you have been healed."
- *Matthew 11:28–29* "Come to me, all who labor and are heavy laden, and I will give you rest."

Prayer

Jesus, thank You for taking my pain seriously. Thank You for bearing the weight of my sin and sorrow. I rest (yes you can take rest) today in Your healing grace and peace.

Field Note

Sharon Ann Lane, an Army combat nurse served in Chu Lai, Vietnam treating wounded soldiers in the heat of a combat zone. She was killed in a rocket attack in 1969 while trying to protect her patients from incoming indirect fire earning her the bronze star with a V device for valor. (National Museum of the United States Army, n.d.) She offered healing in a place of destruction. Her sacrifice reminds us that healing and suffering often stand side by side. Like Christ, she entered the chaos to bring peace to those hurting and wounded and through His sacrifice those who do good works to help heal as He has healed us, will live on with Him in Heaven.

WEEK 5 † TRUST AND DIRECTION

Key Verse: *Proverbs 3:5-6 (ESV)*

> **"Trust in the Lord with all your heart, and do not lean on your own understanding. In all your ways acknowledge Him, and He will make straight your paths."**

Day 1

Mission Insight

I'll admit this has developed into one of my favorite Proverbs. This popular proverb offers guidance in a world full of uncertainty. For service members who are used to plans, procedures, and orders, the idea of releasing control can feel unnatural. In uniform, we often trust in structure and chain of command, but whereas civilian life can feel less organized, more ambiguous. God calls us to a different kind of trust, one that depends not on our understanding, but on His wisdom and presence. Acknowledging Him isn't just about Sunday prayers; it's about daily decisions. And when we walk that way, He promises to lead us clearly, even if the terrain is new, unfamiliar, or uncertain.

Personal Inspection

Is your life's direction decided by your own compass or through the bold trust of God's guidance?

Prayer
Lord, help me release the need to have it all figured out. Teach me to trust You with my whole heart and follow wherever You lead, for You are truly in command.

Day 2

Mission Insight
Military training often develops confidence in knowing a way to do something, but Proverbs teaches that true wisdom starts with surrender, a common theme you'll read throughout this devotional. When we lean too heavily on what *we* know be it our experience, culturally influenced desires, or worldly logic, we risk missing God's better path. Trusting doesn't come naturally or easily; we can practice it in those moments when we could take control but choose to listen to God first and follow his instruction; Proverbs shows us that it WILL work out for the best.

Personal Inspection
What situation are you tempted to manage on your own instead of surrendering to God?

Prayer
Father, help me let go of my need for control and rely instead on Your greater (The Greatest) wisdom.

Day 3

Mission Insight
Transitioning into or even just navigating civilian life while still wearing the uniform can feel discombobulating, like navigating in a fog or haze. Career changes, identity shifts, and cultural clashes can

overwhelm, but this verse reminds us we're not directionless, we just need to shift our compass and do an azimuth check. Acknowledging God isn't about having every answer; it's about inviting Him into every step and letting him ultimately show us our direction.

Personal Inspection
Why are you not sure which path to take, where do you need to invite God's direction right now?

Prayer
God, walk with me through the uncertainties of this season. Make my path clear in ways I couldn't predict.

Day 4

Mission Insight
Sometimes the hardest part of trust is the part that requires us to be patient. Those of us who swore an oath to defend our nation are used to action, but we are also used to hurry up and wait; spiritual trust sometimes requires stillness, patience, and faith that God is moving even when we don't see it. Trusting God with all your heart means not bolting when the answers don't come fast or on your timeline.

Personal Inspection
How do you usually respond when God's timing feels slow and how has this undue haste made waste?

Prayer
Lord, teach me to wait with trust, not anxiety. Help me remember patience while You're working, even when I can't see the outcome.

Day 5

Mission Insight
Acknowledging God "in all your ways" means nothing is too small to bring to Him. Decisions about money, relationships, time, retirement, and even vacation plans all fall under this umbrella. It's not about checking in with God just on big life events, it's about inviting Him into the ordinary of every single day.

Personal Inspection
What part of your daily life have you kept God out of, unintentionally or otherwise?

Prayer
Jesus, I want You in every part of my day. Help me remember You care about the details, that your voice calls out to guide me on the big and the small events in my life.

Day 6

Mission Insight
God's promise to "make straight your paths" doesn't mean life will be easy it means He'll lead with purpose. Even if the route winds through suffering or setbacks, we're not lost! Every path God clears for us moves toward His goodness, and at the finish line let us hear these words, "Well done, good and faithful servant".

Personal Inspection
How has God used a hard season in your past to move you forward?

Prayer
Lord, thank You for being a God who leads me, not leaves me. Make my path clear and give me courage that I know I possess, to walk it.

Day 7 After-Action Reflection

This week reminded us that trust isn't passive, it's an intentional choice to stop relying on what we can calculate and start depending on the One who sees the whole picture. God doesn't promise ease, but He does promise direction. Whether you're facing a decision, a transition, or simply feeling lost, the guidance remains the same, trust Him with your whole heart. He will make the way forward.

Auxiliary Scriptures

- *Jeremiah 29:11* "For I know the plans I have for you…"
- *Psalm 25:4–5* "Make me to know your ways, O Lord; teach me your paths."

Prayer

God, I trust You with my today and my tomorrow. Lead me not just where I want to go, but where You know I should be.

Field Note

General Norman Schwarzkopf, the Commanding General during Operation Desert Storm (who years later I was fortunate to meet as a Cadet and was gracious enough to give of his time), was known not only for his tactical genius and for not being afraid to take calculated risks; but also for his willingness to pause and reflect before making big decisions at the cost of Soldiers' lives. (Broder 1991) His leadership reminds us that direction isn't always about speed, it's about clarity, conviction, and purpose. Like Proverbs 3:5–6, it takes wisdom to wait, humility to seek counsel, and trust to follow where God leads even when the map isn't fully drawn.

WEEK 6 † TRANSFORMATION

Key Verse: *Romans 12:2 (ESV)*

"Do not be conformed to this world, but be transformed by the renewal of your mind, that by testing you may discern what is the will of God, what is good and acceptable and perfect."

Day 1

Mission Insight

Paul's challenge in Romans 12:2 is both countercultural and deeply hopeful. Instead of blending into the patterns of the world: violence, pride, fear, bitterness, materialism, we're invited into transformation through renewed thinking. For those of us who have spent a career or as a formative young adult adapting to rigid structured systems, combat, or other high operational tempo realities; civilian life can feel disorienting. But God does not ask for blind adjustment, He offers transformation from the inside out through Scripture, prayer, and community; to rewire our minds, reshape our hearts, and renew our spirit.

Personal Inspection

In an honest admission, do you view and judge yourself as the world assesses you or how God does?

Prayer

Lord, I do not want to be shaped by the worldly brokenness around me. Transform me though Your word, Your Spirit from within, and help me live according to Your will.

Day 2

Mission Insight

The world at times encourages self-promotion, revenge, greed, and independence. But God's kingdom turns that upside down and Jesus made the message very clear. Transformation doesn't mean abandoning your identity it means letting God refine it and live in a way that is pleasing to Him, not our culture. Serving means learning adaptability and knowing what it is to take on a new mindset for a mission. In Christ, the mission is lifelong and never too late to take up; becoming more like Him, and less like the world.

Personal Inspection

What worldly mindset have you carried that God may be asking you to release so He can be heard?

Prayer

God, show me the beliefs I have had and ways I've lived that don't come from You. Renew my mind with Your truth in their place.

Day 3

Mission Insight

Transformation, transition, or general change is often accompanied by some form of growing pains or trials. It challenges your comfort zones, habits, and long-held beliefs. But it's also freeing and exciting. We who've lived through a pattern of life shaped by our military profession, more so than Christ over time, may see it as a greater challenge then it is. Renewal doesn't erase the past, but it reframes it, it gives new breath to a new way in your life, a new beginning. Through Christ, healing and growth is possible!

Self-Refection:
What thought pattern do you want God to redeem and renew?

Prayer
Lord, bring light into the darkest corners of my thinking. Heal what's broken and reshape it with hope.

Day 4

Mission Insight
The military teaches situational awareness, being alert to your surroundings. God teaches spiritual awareness and being alert to what shapes your thinking; just as you were on the lookout for physical threats, God wants you to look out for spiritual ones. Spiritual warfare is real, forces of evil through cultural delivery, media, politics, bitterness, even pride, can all creep in unnoticed. Paul urges us to pay attention and be cognizant asking, are we being formed by the world or by the WORD?

Personal Inspection
What are you feeding your mind with daily, and is it leading to transformation or conformity?

Prayer
Jesus, sharpen my awareness. Help me guard my mind and fill it not with what life brings, but rather with what brings life.

Day 5

Mission Insight

Sometimes transformation begins with one hard decision: forgiving someone, telling the truth, setting a new habit, giving yourself to the Lord. Renewal doesn't happen by accident, it happens through intent and obedience. Each time we choose God's way over our own, the Spirit does quiet, powerful work inside us; and though we surrender ourselves, we truly are gaining our freedom.

Personal Inspection

What step of obedience is God calling you to today as part of your transformation?

Prayer

Father, I want to obey even when it's uncomfortable. Shape me with each small step of faithfulness and let me see how giving to you is truly gaining for me.

Day 6

Mission Insight

Discerning God's will can feel mysterious or even overwhelming, if you're like me, in your studies you have realized there is so much to take in. But Paul connects this learning to transformation; when your mind is renewed, your heart becomes aligned with God's desires. It's not just about hearing a voice and reading words it's about becoming a person who knows what pleases God because you know His heart. Jesus left us with the Holy Spirit, it's in you; trust that you know more than you give yourself credit.

Personal Inspection

Where do you need God's guidance and how might a renewed mind help you discern it?

Prayer

Lord, I want to know Your will. Transform my mind so I can see clearly and walk confidently in You.

Day 7 After-Action Reflection

This week has invited us into a different kind of change, not cosmetic, but to our core. God doesn't just want behavior modification; He wants heart transformation. All of us regardless of our walks of life or careers can get stuck in survival mode, but Christ calls us into a life of renewal. As your mind is reshaped by truth, you'll begin to walk in God's will; not out of obligation, but in the freedom only He can provide. Transformation is a lifelong process, but every step brings you closer to Christ's likeness.

Auxiliary Scriptures

- *Ephesians 4:22–24* "Put off your old self… and be renewed in the spirit of your minds."
- *2 Corinthians 5:17* "If anyone is in Christ, he is a new creation…"

Prayer

Jesus, keep renewing my mind and transforming my heart. Let my life reflect the power of Your Spirit at work within me.

Field Note

The 12 Disciples of Jesus underwent a radical transformation after the resurrection, and the Holy Spirit was poured out on them

(Acts 2). Before that moment, many had fled in fear (Mark 14:50), denied Christ (John 18:25–27), or hid behind locked doors (John 20:19). But when the Spirit came upon them, they were no longer conformed to fear or uncertainty, they were transformed in purpose and courage. Peter, once afraid to admit knowing Jesus, boldly preached the gospel to thousands in Jerusalem that same day, and the Church was born. From that moment on, the disciples traveled throughout the known world proclaiming Christ. Their minds had been renewed by the Spirit's call to self-sacrifice and proclamation. (Crossway Bibles 2016) Their story is the living embodiment of Romans 12:2, lives transformed by the Spirit, launching a movement that would reshape history.

WEEK 7 † PEACE BEYOND UNDERSTANDING

Key Verse: *Philippians 4:6-7 (ESV)*

"Do not be anxious about anything, but in everything by prayer and supplication with thanksgiving let your requests be made known to God. And the peace of God, which surpasses all understanding, will guard your hearts and your minds in Christ Jesus."

Day 1

Mission Insight

These verses are among some of the most quoted for a reason, they speak directly to addressing the restless human spirit. If you belong to the fraternity of "military personnel" you know anxiety differently than most; it can come from the battlefield, the return/leaving home, the weight of responsibility, or the chaos of change. Paul doesn't say, "Don't feel anxious." He says bring that anxiety to God, through honest prayer, genuine need, and gratitude. When we do, something powerful happens; peace that may not make sense otherwise, arrives. For veterans and civilian alike, God's peace is real, available, and it is stronger than fear.

Personal Inspection

We all endure anxiety, when is the last time you reacted first with prayer and thanks to God in response?

Prayer

Lord, I bring You the anxiety I try to hide. Help me turn to You in everything and protect my heart with Your peace.

Day 2

Mission Insight

Anxiety can sneak in through worry over finances, health, or family. Former and current military often struggle with control, when you're trained to anticipate a superior's needs, a subordinate requests, enemy threats, and be ready to adapt at split seconds notice, it's hard to release control to God. But Paul says peace comes <u>after</u> surrender, not before. When you finally give the anxiety to God, He replaces it with peace.

Personal Inspection

What are you still trying to control or worry about that God is inviting you to release?

Prayer

Father, I don't want to carry what You never asked me to hold by myself. Help me release it today.

Day 3

Mission Insight

Prayer isn't just about asking, it's also about giving thanks. Gratitude shifts our perspective from scarcity to abundance. Even in combat zones I still remember being thankful and sharing that thanks in prayer, be it for another day, the Soldiers I served with, for protection, and my family back home. Gratitude and acknowledgement of God and all his workings in your life to help carry your burdens, opens the door to peace even in the toughest of places.

Personal Inspection

What can you thank God for, even while you're still waiting on answers or in challenging times?

Prayer

Lord, thank You for what I already have. Teach me to see Your goodness even in the hard places.

Day 4

Mission Insight

Peace is more than a feeling it's protection and acknowledgement of security. Paul describes it as a guard, posted over your heart and mind. In Christ, peace is not passive. It's aggressive, proactive, defending you from the enemy's passive whispers or full-frontal assault on your spirit…you are protected!

Personal Inspection

Where do you need God's peace to post up and protect your thoughts?

Prayer

Jesus, be my Defender today. Let Your peace shield me where I feel vulnerable or where evil attacks.

Day 5

Mission Insight

Not all anxiety is irrational, sometimes there's real danger, real loss, real reasons to worry. Paul doesn't dismiss reality; he knew a variety of challenging realities better than most as we read in the book of Acts. He just invites us to move through it with God instead of alone. Prayer is where we remember we're not abandoned and peace is where God reminds us we're not defeated.

Personal Inspection

What anxiety do you need to talk to God about honestly (admitting what He already knows), without filters?

Prayer

Lord, here's what's really going on. I trust You enough to be honest. Please meet me in this mess.

Day 6

Mission Insight

Mental health matters. For many veterans, anxiety, and post-traumatic stress can be long battles. But this verse doesn't promise the absence of struggle it promises God's nearness and peace in the middle of it. Seeking help is not weakness; it's wisdom. Prayer and therapy, faith and support, they work together.

Personal Inspection

What step toward peace are you avoiding because it feels vulnerable or you are struggling with humility?

Prayer

God, help me seek what I need without shame. Use every tool to bring peace into my life.

Day 7 After-Action Reflection

This week, we've been reminded that peace isn't earned it's received. It's the result of trust, gratitude, and honest prayer. Paul knew anxiety. He wrote these words to the church in Philippi from imprisonment in Rome; yet still, he points us to a peace that defies logic, a peace that protects us. In uniform or out, we all need that kind of peace. And it is available today, right now, in Christ.

Auxiliary Scriptures

- *John 14:27* "Peace I leave with you; my peace I give to you…"
- *Isaiah 26:3* "You keep him in perfect peace whose mind is stayed on You…"

Prayer

Jesus, thank You for peace that makes no sense apart from You. I receive it now as You guard my heart and mind today with Your perfect presence.

Field Note

Army nurse Lieutenant Annie G. Fox was serving at Hickam Field, Hawaii, when the Japanese attacked Pearl Harbor on December 7, 1941. Amid chaos, casualties, and bombardment, Lt. Fox remained calm, directing evacuations, managing patient triage, and caring for the wounded under fire. For her actions, she became the first woman in American history to receive the Purple Heart (later changed to a Bronze Star). (The Bravery of Army Nurse Annie G. Fox at Pearl Haror", n.d.) Her steadiness came not from a lack of fear, but from her commitment and peace under pressure. Like Philippians 4:6–7 promises, she demonstrated a peace that defied logic, guarding her heart and mind through service and courage in the storm.

WEEK 8 † POWER, LOVE, AND SELF-CONTROL

Key Verse: *2 Timothy 1:7 (ESV)*

"For God gave us a spirit not of fear but of power and love and self-control."

Day 1

Mission Insight

Paul wrote this to Timothy, a young leader likely facing fear, opposition, and the pressure of spiritual responsibility. The reminder is sharp, fear doesn't come from God. What does? Power, love, and self-control. These aren't just virtues, they're spiritual tools. We've been trained in strength and self-control, but yet fear still lingers: fear of failure, rejection, the future, or even fear of memories. This verse reorients us, we've been equipped not just for the battlefield, but for life with God. Fear may knock, but it doesn't own us. God's Spirit is inside us, powerful, steady, capable, and anchored in love.

Personal Inspection

Do you remind yourself daily, no matter the world throws at you, that God gave you the tools you need to overcome whatever may come your way?

Prayer
Lord, help me recognize fear for what it is and reject it in Your name. Fill me with Your power, love, and self-control so that I may overcome it all.

Day 2

Mission Insight
Fear often distorts reality. It tells you you're not ready, not worthy, not capable. But God's Spirit says otherwise. God's power reminds you that you're equipped for this life. Love reminds you that you're never alone. And self-control reminds you that your response is stronger than your fear.

Personal Inspection
What fear is currently speaking louder than God's truth, how are you going to change that right now?

Prayer
God, silence the lies I've believed. Help me live from the Truth, and the Spirit You've placed in me.

Day 3

Mission Insight
Power without love can be dangerous. Love without self-control can be chaotic. But when all three come together, they reflect the character of Christ. Served? Means we are service members living in extremes, with high demands, high adrenaline, and high emotion. But the Spirit offers balance: boldness with compassion, discipline with grace.

Personal Inspection
Which of the three: power, love, or self-control do you need more of today to find balance?

Prayer
Lord, shape me to reflect all of who You are. Grow these gifts in me through Your Spirit.

Day 4

Mission Insight
Timothy may have been intimidated by the challenges before him, like most people I certainly haven't been immune to this myself. Paul didn't dismiss the fear, he changed the perspective. He reminded Timothy that God had already given him everything he needed. Even after all you have done you may not feel brave, you may not feel qualified. However, never forget the Spirit in you is not fearful, it is strong.

Personal Inspection
Where do you feel unqualified and how might God already be or already have equipped you?

Prayer
Jesus, I don't always feel capable. But You've given me what I need. Help me rely on Your Spirit, not my feelings that have held me back in the past; today is a new beginning.

Day 5

Mission Insight
Self-control is often overlooked but it's a sign of spiritual maturity. Whether you're an old warhorse or a new recruit you face unique

social temptations: anger, isolation, addiction, or numbing behaviors. But the Spirit offers not just conviction over these but control. Not from our sheer willpower alone, but from His grace working inside us; His will, His power.

Personal Inspection
What area of your life needs more self-control rooted in the Spirit, not in shame or coping?

Prayer
God, give me strength to choose what's good for my body, mind, and spirit. Empower me to walk in discipline that honors You and reflects Your will.

Day 6

Mission Insight
Love changes everything. In a military culture that prizes toughness, love can feel like a vulnerability or just not the expression of choice. But Christ-centered love is a weapon against fear, hatred, and despair. It builds bridges where conflict and destruction once stood, and the ability to be compassionate. You were not given a weak spirit; you were given love as your foundation from which all else should flow.

Personal Inspection
Who in your life needs to experience the love of Christ through you?

Prayer
Jesus, make me a person who loves courageously. Let fear fall away where love takes root.

Day 7 After-Action Reflection

Fear may follow us, but it doesn't lead us. This week reminded us that God's Spirit empowers us with strength for every battle, love for every relationship, and self-control for every struggle. You were not given a spirit of fear but of purpose, dignity, and grace. Whether you served in war or are fighting battles within, God is still writing your story and His love is the pen and ink He uses to write your story.

Auxiliary Scriptures

- *Joshua 1:9* "Be strong and courageous… the Lord your God is with you…"
- *Romans 8:15* "You did not receive a spirit of slavery to fall back into fear…"

Prayer

God, I reject the spirit of fear in Jesus' name. Fill me again with Your power, Your love, and Your control. Let me live boldly and freely in You.

Field Note

General Sam Houston, commander of the Texan Army during its war for independence from Mexico and later President of the Republic of Texas, lived for years as a womanizer and heavy drinker, even named "Big Drunk" by the Cherokees. Houston's alcoholism nearly destroyed his public and personal life. But after marrying Margaret Lea in 1840, a devout Christian, Houston underwent a dramatic transformation. Influenced by her faith and the gospel, he was baptized in 1854, publicly declaring his faith in Jesus Christ. Houston gave up drinking, became a steady statesman, and spoke often of his trust in God. (Houston 2022) Houston's story is a true account of God replacing a life of self-destruction with power, love, and a sound mind just as Paul describes in 2 Timothy 1:7.

WEEK 9 † REST FOR THE WEARY

Key Verse: *Matthew 11:28-30 (ESV)*

"Come to me, all who labor and are heavy laden, and I will give you rest. Take my yoke upon you, and learn from me, for I am gentle and lowly in heart, and you will find rest for your souls. For my yoke is easy, and my burden is light."

Day 1

Mission Insight

Jesus offers something no commander, no counselor, no system can provide as equally…rest for the soul. These words are not advocating laziness, they're for the emotionally burdened, the overworked, the exhausted. Regardless of our branch of service we all tend to carry packs full of anxiety, stress from responsibility, regrets, life challenges, or trauma. Jesus doesn't say, "Drop it and move on." He says, "Bring it to Me." His yoke isn't about more weight; it's about shared weight. We still move forward, but no longer alone, and with his power carrying the heavy load. Because of this true rest begins not just physically, but deep within.

Personal Inspection

How is your soul labored and heavy laden, have you thought to genuinely ask God to carry it for you?

Prayer
Jesus, I bring You the burdens I have carried too long. Teach me how to walk with You, rest in You, and trust You to take these burdens from me and bring peace.

Day 2

Mission Insight
Many veterans never fully stop moving. Even after service ends, the pace continues, mentally, emotionally, and spiritually we march on trained in execution and mission accomplishment…are you still 15 minutes early to everything (if you are still serving, yes still be 15 minutes early to everything!)? But Jesus does not rush us. He calls us to rest with Him, not just from something, but to know all things in this world can be put on his shoulders. His rest is not an escape or passing the buck it's restoration in our soul with a new perspective on how to deal with our burdens.

Personal Inspection
Where have you confused rest with inactivity and how might Jesus be inviting you into a deeper kind of rest?

Prayer
Lord, slow my steps and quiet my mind. Let me find true rest and peace in Your presence.

Day 3

Mission Insight
"Take my yoke upon you" sounds like more responsibility but it's actually about partnership. A yoke binds two together to share the load. Jesus is not giving us more work He's offering to carry it with us

and his yoke is light. His strength makes the burden bearable, he will do the heavy lifting all you have to do is trust Him to carry it and see what happens; you will be amazed at the peace you'll have within.

Personal Inspection
What would it look like for you to stop carrying things alone, have you asked yourself why you are carrying it alone, when you do not have to?

Prayer
Jesus, join me in the weight I am carrying. Teach me how to let You share the burden, teach me how to let go of control, surrender to you, and in turn find myself free.

Day 4

Mission Insight
The world prizes hustle, strength, and performance; if we didn't Olympic athletes wouldn't end up on Wheaties boxes. Jesus however values gentleness and humility in our life's performance as well, and in turn the courage to do so he considers a strength. For many, showing a perceived weakness feels unsafe therefore we never allow ourselves rest. However, Jesus doesn't judge us by the world's assessment of our performance, but in our performance to and for him, one that also comes with rest and peace as well.

Personal Inspection
How have you misunderstood Jesus' heart and how can you trust His gentleness today?

Prayer
Lord, help me trust that You won't reject my weariness. You are gentle and kind, let me learn that to live in such a way will bring me peace, rest, and a whole new strength I've never fully known.

Day 5

Mission Insight

Many of our burdens aren't from God. They're self-imposed: expectations, guilt, perfectionism, substance abuse, cultural infatuations, or trying to fix others. Jesus didn't hand you that load, we have decided to go against his teaching and our own hearts to bring these burdens upon ourselves. He's asking you to trade it for something lighter, something rooted in grace; he will us these unforced errors to bring you to Him, that you can be sure; not to punish you but to take these burdens from you and give you a better life.

Personal Inspection

What burden are you carrying that Jesus never asked you to bear, in what ways are you letting you hold yourself back, how are they stifling you from your true purpose and potential?

Prayer

Father, help me lay down the false burdens I've taken on. Teach me to carry only what You give, live in contentment with your gifts, and realize that life will bring me greater joy than anything I've introduced.

Day 6

Mission Insight

True rest can't be found in numbing out or running away. It comes through intimacy with Jesus. As we walk beside Him, learn His ways, trust His timing, follow His voice, we will experience rest and peace, even when the world remains hard and chaotic.

Personal Inspection

How can walking with Jesus bring rest in your current season even if your circumstances don't change?

Prayer
Jesus, keep me close to You. Let every step with You lead me closer to peace.

Day 7 After-Action Reflection

This week reminds us that Jesus doesn't only save us, He sustains us. Rest isn't a luxury in the Christian life it's a necessity and a given blessing. Many who serve/served never learned how to rest, but now, in Christ, you can. You don't have to keep proving yourself or carrying everything alone. He invites you gently, and personally to come, rest, and walk with Him.

Auxiliary Scriptures

- *Psalm 23:1–3* "He makes me lie down in green pastures…"
- *Hebrews 4:9–10* "There remains a rest for the people of God…"

Prayer
Jesus, I receive Your invitation to rest, calm my heart, slow my mind, and restore my soul as I walk with You.

Field Note

General Dwight D. Eisenhower during WWII once said: "Plans are worthless, but planning is everything." (National Archives 2019) He understood the toll of constant strain and decision-making. Behind the scenes, he carved out moments to breath and pray, like on the mountaintop overlooking Malta prior to the assault on Sicily, because sustained leadership requires pause, and rest in our faith. (Smith 2024) Like Jesus' invitation in Matthew 11, Eisenhower knew that leading well requires space to lay down burdens even for a moment, and trust that God carries what we cannot.

WEEK 10 † ENDURANCE THROUGH TRIALS

Key Verse: *James 1:2-4 (ESV)*

"Count it all joy... when you meet trials of various kinds, for you know that the testing of your faith produces steadfastness. And let steadfastness have its full effect, that you may be perfect and complete, lacking in nothing."

Day 1

Mission Insight
James doesn't sugarcoat reality, He speaks to people who are in the trial. And instead of offering an escape, He offers perspective; trials aren't wasted, they're productive. We know the rigors of being tested be it boot camp, combat, training exercises, developmental schools, etc., they are challenges to facilitate growth. The pain may be real, but so is the purpose. Life's trials are much the same, producing a resilience rooted in faith from choosing to trust God in difficulty. The result? A stronger believer and faith that holds under pressure as we serve the purpose God has meant for us.

Personal Inspection
How do you react to life's trials; do you accept God's purpose in them or are you missing the connection?

Prayer
God, I don't enjoy the trials, but I want to trust You in them. I know you are growing something deep in me that only adversity can shape.

Day 2

Mission Insight
Joy and trials belonging in the same sentence (no pain, no gain)? But James isn't talking about joy being based on the pain of trials; its joy based on knowing God is doing something through it and the transformation within you. When you serve (d), every crucible you endured along the way made you better, mentally stronger, more resilient, more capable at your job; God is working the same way in you.

Personal Inspection
Where in your life is God calling you to find joy not in the trial, but in what it's producing?

Prayer
Lord, help me find joy in knowing You're with me and working, even when it hurts.

Day 3

Mission Insight
Like those many dreaded evaluations and inspections you've endured having spent any amount of time in the service; God's spiritual trials reveal what's already inside us, where our strength and weaknesses are. When things fall apart it's a litmus test and we discover if our confidence is in God, in something else, or maybe nothing at all.

James reminds us, faith is not just belief, it's trust and a steadfastness in God when under pressure that will deliver us more so than anything else.

Personal Inspection

What recent test has shown you something about your faith, good or bad?

Prayer

God, show me where I stand with You, not to shame me, but to strengthen me where I am weak.

Day 4

Mission Insight

Steadfastness isn't passive. It's active endurance, showing up, pressing on, choosing to believe again. It's the quiet strength that refuses to quit, that you can't be knocked down, that you will never retreat! Many seasoned vets have seen this firsthand, endurance in deployments, in hardship, in loss. James is saying that same grit, when rooted in Christ, leads to deep transformation.

Personal Inspection

Where are you being called to persevere when quitting would be easier?

Prayer

Lord, give me strength to stay the course and never surrender. I don't want to give up, I refuse to give up, grow me through this.

Day 5

Mission Insight

Endurance doesn't just build character, it brings completion. James says that when steadfastness finishes its work, we become mature, "lacking nothing." That's God's goal, not ease, but depth. He's not punishing us out of spite He's preparing us. And He's with us through every step; remember Jesus has asked nothing of you that He did not ask of himself.

Personal Inspection

What trial in your past shaped you into someone stronger or wiser?

Prayer

God, thank You for staying with me in every season. Keep maturing me, even when it's uncomfortable so that I may serve my purpose in your Kingdom's greater plan.

Day 6

Mission Insight

Veterans often return from service experiences changed, and not always for the bad. Some changes are hard at the time but the results are net positive. God uses trials and adversity not to destroy but to rebuild and make new. In His hands, trials become tools, not weapons. James invites us to see the bigger picture, what feels like breaking may be shaping and strengthening, like a blacksmith forges steel with fire.

Personal Inspection

What current struggle might be part of God's rebuilding process in your life?

Prayer
Father, I trust that You are shaping me. Use even this trial to form something beautiful in me.

Day 7 After-Action Reflection

James calls us to a faith that endures, not escapes. This week reminded us that our trials are not just obstacles, they are opportunities. God is more interested in our growth than our constant comfort. And in the trial, He gives us Himself. Endurance, when rooted in faith, leads to maturity, depth, and dependence on the One who never fails. You have faced hardship before. You can face this too, with God at your side.

Auxiliary Scriptures

- *Romans 5:3–5* "Suffering produces endurance… and hope does not disappoint."
- *Hebrews 12:11* "No discipline seems pleasant at the time, but painful…"

Prayer
God, thank You that no pain is wasted in Your hands. Help me endure with hope, grow with grace, and trust that You are completing what You started in me.

Field Note

The Bataan Death March in 1942, over 75 thousand American and Filipino POWs were forced to march over 60 miles with little food or water, with thousands dying or killed along the way. Survivors didn't endure by strength alone, many endured through faith, brotherhood, and doing what they had to do in the mists of what faced them. Their pain forged a resilience the enemy couldn't break, a faith in God and each other that carried on beyond the war. (Herrick 2012) James 1:2–4 reminds us that our suffering can be met with the same faith as these men, through a God who grows us even in trial. Like those Soldiers, we press on not because it's easy, but because we are being shaped for something greater and have their example to follow.

WEEK 11 † GOD IS NEAR THE BROKEN-HEARTED

Key Verse: *Psalm 34:18 (ESV)*

"The Lord is near to the brokenhearted and saves the crushed in spirit."

Day 1

Mission Insight

This verse offers comfort without condition and tell us God is not repelled by brokenness. For those of us who often carry burdens few can see or understand, this truth is a saving grace. There are seasons when strength runs out, the weight is too much, and you feel isolated in the struggle. However, David in Psalm 34:18 declares something radical; God comes close in those very moments! He doesn't abandon us, He steps into our sorrow, dwells with the crushed, and offers rescue not just from situations but also from emotional despair. His closeness is the first step toward healing.

Personal Inspection

Do you acknowledge daily that God is near, that He is in you, or do forget to say hi to the one who is closest to you and never leaves you to take on this world alone?

Prayer

Lord, I feel the weight of things too heavy to carry alone. Remind me that You are near, You aren't leaving, healing begins in You.

Day 2

Mission Insight
To be brokenhearted can find us in many forms and many ways: grief, regret, disappointment, loss. You and I may carry the pain of what was lost overseas or back home. God's nearness doesn't erase the pain, but it honors it, recognizes it, and brings it into the light. He comes close not to necessarily fix us quickly and conveniently, but to hold us faithfully, bring us comfort, and heal us fully while providing both strength and peace in the process.

Personal Inspection
What part of your story still feels broken and how can you invite God into that space?

Prayer
God, I don't need a quick fix. I need Your presence. Come close to the places I still ache and with you I shall overcome.

Day 3

Mission Insight
We often hide our pain to appear strong, but Scripture flips the script. God doesn't draw near to the put together, but to the crushed. Real strength begins in surrender; he already knows hiding the pain only hurts you. When you finally allow yourself to grieve, to feel, to

cry out; God meets you there. He's ready, waiting on you to let Him in and with Him you'll be stronger than ever before!

Personal Inspection

What have you been trying to manage alone instead of surrendering it to God as he wants?

Prayer

Jesus, I lay down the mask of strength because I know you won't judge me. Meet me where I really am, not where I pretend to be and lead me to where we should be together.

Day 4

Mission Insight

The battlefield doesn't end when deployment does. Many combat veterans return with silent wounds, like moral injury, guilt, and altered mental states. But Psalm 34:18 speaks into that silence. Crushed in spirit? God's on His way...actually, He is already here! You're not too broken for Him, you're exactly the one He moves toward; He is literally a first responder for your heart and your spirit.

Personal Inspection

What guilt or shame are you still carrying that God is ready to meet with mercy?

Prayer

Jesus, You are not afraid of my pain, You already know it and are still here with me. Help me believe You came for the broken, not the perfect.

Day 5

Mission Insight

Sometimes we feel God is also far because of abandonment by friends, family, or even fellow soldiers who left us feeling like all will betray us or can't be trusted. But God is not like them. He doesn't walk away when things get messy. His nearness isn't conditional it's assured, just as Jesus promised to not lose one of us give to him by the Father (John 6:39) he will not lose you.

Personal Inspection

Whose absence have you mistaken for God's and how might He be drawing near even now?

Prayer

God, help me separate human failure from Your faithfulness. Thank You that You never leave me, even if I am lost you will surely always be with me.

Day 6

Mission Insight

Remember from Week 4 we learned you don't have to "get better" to be near to God. His rescue often begins while we're still crushed. Sometimes the greatest healing comes not from escaping the pain, but from knowing we're not alone in it. His Presence, not your perfection, is God's response to heartbreak.

Personal Inspection

Where can you stop striving and simply let God sit with you in the pain and let Him work?

Prayer

Lord, I don't need answers right now…I need You. Be near to me. Through Your works I will learn that is enough.

Day 7 After-Action Reflection

This week reminded us that God is not a distant observer He is a present comforter. For the brokenhearted, the crushed in spirit, the weary and grieving, this verse isn't sentiment it's God's survival guide. God doesn't shame us for being low. He draws near, He stays, and He saves. No matter what the cause of your brokenness, you are not beyond His reach. You are exactly where He promises to be.

Auxiliary Scriptures

- *Isaiah 61:1* "He has sent me to bind up the brokenhearted…"
- *Matthew 5:4* "Blessed are those who mourn, for they shall be comforted."

Prayer

God, thank You that You come near when everyone else walks away. Stay with me through the dark places. Let Your presence be my strength and my hope.

Field Note

Army Chaplain Darren Turner, whose story later inspired a movie, in 2007 deployed to Iraq with the mission of caring for Soldiers souls. But after months in combat zones, he returned broken himself, struggling with trauma, anger, and selfishness. It was through embracing his own issues, and allowing God to meet him in them, that healing began. (Jackson and Jackson 2019) Psalm 34:18 was not just a comfort—it became a lifeline. Like Turner, many veterans find that healing begins not with trying harder, but with letting God be close when you're at your lowest.

WEEK 12 † STRENGTH TO ENDURE

Key Verse: *Isaiah 40:31 (ESV)*

"But they who wait for the Lord shall renew their strength; they shall mount up with wings like eagles; they shall run and not be weary; they shall walk and not faint."

Day 1

Mission Insight

This promise comes after a long reminder in Isaiah that human strength eventually runs out, but God's doesn't. Serving in any capacity you understand fatigue: physical, emotional, and spiritual. Whether it's the long grind of deployment or the slow recovery of reintegration, strength wears thin. But Isaiah offers hope not in pushing harder, but in waiting better. Waiting doesn't mean idleness, it means trust in God's timeline Those who wait on the Lord find new strength that lifts them, sustains them, and enables them to keep going when their own reserves are gone. Isaiah tells us to hold on, that God is on His way in our life and the power from it will be amazing!

Personal Inspection

Do you project your limitations onto God having the same, do you truly realize His strength is limitless?

Prayer

God, You know how tired I am. Teach me how to wait on You, and renew my strength for what's ahead.

Day 2

Mission Insight

Military culture often celebrates the one who pushes through, powers ahead, and never stops. But this verse teaches us that real endurance comes from a different source, waiting on God. Strength isn't always proven by speed, it's proven by staying power in faith, to let God work instead of being impatient and trying to do it all ourselves.

Personal Inspection

Where are you trying to push through on your own strength instead of waiting on God's?

Prayer

Lord, I have been powering ahead alone, trying to do it my way, tiring myself out. Help me pause and draw strength from You instead and live your way so that I may soar.

Day 3

Mission Insight

"Mount up with wings like eagles..." what a picture. Eagles soar not by flapping harder, but by catching the current. God's strength is like that, lifting us when we align with Him, not when we exhaust ourselves. Veterans need that kind of lift, especially when post-service life or just living in a civilian culture feels like flapping against the wind.

Personal Inspection

What would it look like to let God lift you instead of you lifting yourself, what would the heights God would help you achieve look like?

Prayer

Father, I have been flapping in my own effort too often ignoring what You've given me to help me fly to new heights. Help me catch the wind of Your presence and rise again.

Day 4

Mission Insight

Sometimes endurance does not look like soaring. It looks like putting one foot in front of the other. This verse covers it all: flying, running, walking. God meets you whether you are on a mountaintop or low crawling through a mud pit and barbed wire. His promise? You will not faint, you will not lose hope, He is on his way; do not ever give up!

Personal Inspection

What is one area where you feel like giving up and how does this verse speak to enduring instead?

Prayer

Lord, strengthen me for this stretch. I'm tired, but I want to keep walking knowing if I keep just moving forward with You, we will get where You have planned for me.

Day 5

Mission Insight
Again, waiting on God isn't passive, it is active trust. It is choosing not to rush into decisions, not to panic when doors close, not to give in when the future looks uncertain. Front line Soldiers know what it means to hold the line (remember Colonel Chamberlain). Spiritually, waiting means doing just that holding on while God works, keep going with Him, and he will work wonders in your life readying you for the charge ahead.

Personal Inspection
What are you waiting for, and how can you trust God more fully as you wait?

Prayer
Jesus, I surrender my timeline and my need to control. Teach me to trust You while I wait.

Day 6

Mission Insight
Life does not call for just a burst of energy, you need unending endurance. God doesn't just refill your fuel tank with JP8 that will run out way too soon and you have to fill up again (have you been there?). He gives you something better; the warriors who feel burned out by life, work, or stress know this need. God's supply is fresh and never runs out or ever runs dry; a living water to never thirst again (John 4:14).

Personal Inspection
Where do you need more than recovery, where do you need <u>renewal</u>?

Prayer

Lord, I do not just want to get through, I want to be renewed. Remind me and show me how every day is a new opportunity. Fill me with Your life today.

Day 7 After-Action Reflection

This week reminded us that the best strength is strength found in God. God never intended us to live on grit alone. His promise in Isaiah 40:31 isn't about avoiding fatigue, because it's going to happen. Whether you're walking through grief, running toward healing, or needing to rise above it all, God's strength is available. Not just for the fit, but for the weary. Not just for the brave, but for the honest and vulnerable. Wait on Him and watch Him lift you; you will soar!

Auxiliary Scriptures

- *Psalm 27:14* "Wait for the Lord; be strong, and let your heart take courage…"
- *2 Corinthians 12:9* "My grace is sufficient for you, for My power is made perfect in weakness."

Prayer

God, You are my strength when mine is gone. Teach me to wait, to trust, and to rise in Your power.

Field Note

Army Sergeant Brendan Marrocco, a truly inspirational story, survived an IED blast in Iraq in 2009 that left him a quadruple amputee. Through extensive recovery, surgeries, and sheer will, he not only survived but later received a double arm transplant in 2012. ("Army Surgeon General Meets with Double-Arm Transplant Recipient Sgt. Brendan Marrocco" 2013) His story isn't just one of resilience, it's one of renewal. The long wait for restoration was marked by moments of both weakness, and of surprising strength. Like Isaiah 40:31, Brendan's journey is a perfect illustration of when life makes it so we can't move forward on our own, God carries us and will move us forward.

WEEK 13 † PEACE IN THE MIDDLE OF TROUBLE

Key Verse: *John 16:33 (ESV)*

"I have said these things to you, that in me you may have peace. In the world you will have tribulation. But take heart; I have overcome the world."

Day 1

Mission Insight

These are some of Jesus' final words to His disciples before His arrest. He doesn't promise a smooth road, He promises Himself. I know you understand tribulation, both external and internal. Physical injuries, emotional hurts, broken relationships, or transition struggles; these are the real wars many fight after the uniform is hung up or when patches change. Jesus doesn't ignore the reality of suffering. Instead, He offers peace in the midst of it, not apart from it. And then He drops the Mic, "I have overcome the world." Your pain is real, but it's not final! Victory belongs to Him, and peace comes through Him.

Personal Inspection

When facing tribulation do you truly feel and act as if the ultimate Victor and Champion is on your side?

Prayer

Jesus, thank You for being honest about this life. When I face trouble, remind me that You've already overcome it all, and You are with me now and I too shall overcome.

Day 2

Mission Insight

Peace does not mean the absence of struggle it means the presence of Christ. Jesus is clear and says, "You will have tribulation," therefore you should not be surprised when life gives you lemons. However, the key is where we find peace; in Him, not in perfect circumstances. For those like us, this truth reframes everything. Even when the battle rages on, peace is possible, you just have to look in the right places to find it…HIM!

Personal Inspection

Where have you been searching for peace outside of Christ, and how's that working for you?

Prayer

Lord, help me stop chasing peace in the wrong places. Settle me in Your presence and know that You can truly calm the storm.

Day 3

Mission Insight

Jesus says, "Take heart." That is a command to lift your chin, square your shoulders, and remember who you're with. The battle might not be over, but the war is won, and victory is assured. Stand tall knowing you are on the team that won. Especially for the veteran who feels like they are still fighting alone, this verse is a call to courage, rooted in Christ's victory.

Personal Inspection

What would it mean to "take heart" in your current struggle, are you standing tall in Christ?

Prayer

Jesus, lift my spirit when I feel defeated. Remind me that Your victory is my strength.

Day 4

Mission Insight

Some tribulations are loud and explosive such as debilitating loss, visible suffering. Others are quiet; loneliness, depression, hidden wounds. Jesus covers them all. His peace is wide enough for any storm (after all he was pretty good at calming them) and deep enough for every silence. Take heart doesn't mean fake joy it means real courage in the face of adversity knowing that it will be ok, Jesus already won, and in that is peace over the storms!

Personal Inspection

What tribulation are you facing silently, and how can you bring it to Jesus?

Prayer

God, You see what I am going through even when no one else does. Be my peace in the quiet struggle, be my hope trough all trial and tribulation.

Day 5

Mission Insight

The phrase "I have overcome the world" changes everything. Christ's resurrection means the worst thing is never the last thing. That includes death, trauma, shame, and fear. For any of us carrying heavy memories, or current stresses, Jesus' victory is not simply symbolic it's concrete assurance and peace! No matter what you face in this world it isn't the last thing, it will all be left behind as we go to where he has prepared a room for us.

Personal Inspection

How does knowing Jesus has overcome the world change your perspective on your pain, how might it bring you peace?

Prayer

Lord, help me live like Your victory is already mine, even when life still feels like a fight.

Day 6

Mission Insight

Sometimes we think peace comes after the battle; it makes sense, finish the mission and then we can take R&R (Rest and Relaxation) or go into a rest cycle. Jesus flips that 180 degrees; peace can come during it. Through prayer, worship, and Scripture, we are anchored in Him. That doesn't mean we feel calm every moment, it means we are never alone, never without a compass, and all things lead to him. So no matter what is today, we can have peace knowing the guarantee of what comes.

Personal Inspection

What practice or thoughts helps you stay connected to Jesus when life feels chaotic?

Prayer

God, help me turn to You first when things fall apart. Be my constant when everything else shifts.

Day 7 After-Action Reflection

Jesus knew His followers would face serious trouble. So do we. But He also promised something greater, His peace and His victory. This week reminded us that peace is not found in perfect outcomes, but in the presence of a Savior who overcame everything we fear. Tribulation is part of the journey, but peace is part of the promise. Take heart and stand tall, you are not alone and this world is not the end of the story.

Auxiliary Scriptures

- *Romans 8:37* "In all these things we are more than conquerors…"
- *Isaiah 41:10* "Fear not, for I am with you…"

Prayer

Jesus, thank You for peace that holds me in the storm. Let me take heart today not because life is easy, but because You have overcome all things in this world.

Field Note

U.S. Army Chaplain Emil Kapaun served alongside front-line troops during the Korean War, often running into active firefights to rescue wounded soldiers. Captured in 1950, he continued to minister to fellow POWs in a North Korean prison camp. Despite severe conditions, illness, and personal suffering, Kapaun remained a source of calm and hope; praying with prisoners, stealing food for the sick, and tending to the wounded. He died in captivity in 1951 never losing his faith and was posthumously awarded the Medal of Honor in 2013 and titled Venerable by the Catholic church paving the way to Saint hood. ("US Army Chaplain, Korean War POW and Future Saint? Father Emil Kapaun Now 'Venerable' - Catholic Standard" 2025) Like Jesus in John 16:33, Chaplain Kapaun brought peace to others even as he walked through tribulation himself.

WEEK 14 † STAMINA IN DOING GOOD

Key Verse: *Galatians 6:9 (ESV)*

"And let us not grow weary of doing good, for in due season we will reap, if we do not give up."

Day 1

Mission Insight

This verse from Paul is especially useful to those on the edge of burnout. Whether you have been serving, leading, helping, or simply trying to do the right thing, weariness is real. The exhaustion that comes continually having to persevere, be disciplined, and carry burdens, especially when others don't or won't is real. Paul does not deny the fatigue, he acknowledges it and says, "Don't give up." Because the reward is not just in the moment, it's in the season that follows. Faithful living often takes time to show fruit, but God sees and He promises, if you keep going it will not be for nothing.

Personal Inspection

Has knowing God is always there for your good, committed you to always doing good works for Him?

Prayer

Lord, I am tired of pressing forward some days. Strengthen me with your endurance to keep doing good, even when I do not see results in real time.

Day 2

Mission Insight

Doing good can feel thankless especially when no one notices or responds, however that is not why we do good. Whether you are supporting a struggling family member, volunteering, or just trying to hold yourself together, you may wonder if it even matters. Paul says it does and God sees what no one else does. Do good and right and let God handle everything else.

Personal Inspection

Where are you tempted to give up on doing the right thing because it feels unseen?

Prayer

God, remind me that You notice every act of obedience, even when no one else does and my good works are important to you.

Day 3

Mission Insight

In the military, perseverance is trained into you, through training exercises, planned discomfort, repetition, and structure. Civilian life rarely offers that kind of reinforcement; compared to the military it's the wild west. Doing good can feel harder without orders or affirmation. That's why Paul encourages us keep going anyway, God's Spirit is your new strength and reward for persevering in an unstructured and chaotic world.

Self-Reflection

What spiritual muscle is being trained in you through repeated perseverance to do good?

Prayer
Jesus, grow resilience in me, not from pride but from purpose. Help me keep doing good, even when it's hard.

Day 4

Mission Insight
"We will reap" speaks to hope of what's to come from our good works. Not every seed shows growth right away. The multitude of good works you do, be it as a service member, parent, friend, family member will take time to materialize. Us veterans used to seeing measurable results, may struggle with God's slower timelines, but the harvest is coming. The seed is in the ground it will germinate on God's time not ours; don't give up, the rewards are coming.

Personal Inspection
What good work have you started that needs renewed hope to continue?

Prayer
Lord, breathe life into what feels stalled. I trust You to bring a harvest in Your time and by Your will.

Day 5

Mission Insight
Weariness isn't just physical, it's spiritual and mental. When discouragement sets in, it's easy to pull back, numb out, or turn cynical, we all met that one salty non-commissioned officers at the end of their career. But Paul urges the opposite, do not grow weary. It's not about never feeling tired, it's about refusing to let tiredness turn into apathy and stop serving the purpose Christ has for us.

Personal Inspection

How can you recognize the difference between healthy rest and spiritual withdrawal, are you resting or have you withdrawn?

Prayer

God, give me discernment to rest well without quitting. Let my spirit stay engaged in Your work.

Day 6

Mission Insight

You are not alone in your perseverance. Every act of goodness, kindness, honesty, and sacrifice ripples outward. For us who have donned the uniform, this is legacy, your opportunities to have reached so many is truly a unique opportunity our profession provides. Doing good today plants seeds that may bless generations to come. Your steadfastness has kingdom impact; don't underestimate how truly valuable your contributions are no matter at what stage in life you make them.

Personal Inspection

What "good" do you want to leave behind for others to find or pay forward?

Prayer

Father, let my life leave a trail of goodness behind me. Help me sow faith, courage, and hope in others.

Day 7 After-Action Reflection

This week reminded us that doing good isn't always glamorous. It's can even be exhausting. But God doesn't measure success by applause, He measures it by faithfulness. The promise stands, your work is not wasted, God sees. The season to reap will come, so do not give up, rest when needed but don't withdrawal; refocus when you must and always keep going. The harvest is His, make it plentiful oh good and faithful servant.

Auxiliary Scriptures

- *1 Corinthians 15:58* "Be steadfast… knowing that in the Lord your labor is not in vain."
- *Hebrews 12:3* "Consider Him who endured… so that you may not grow weary or fainthearted."

Prayer

Lord, keep me from giving up when things get hard. Help me sow good things with hope and finish well, trusting You with the outcome.

Field Note

The Red Ball Express, during WWII was a convoy system of mostly African American truck drivers who kept supply lines open during the Allied advance after D-Day. Facing long hours, bad roads, and enemy threats, they pressed on day and night. Their perseverance and dedication were mostly unsung; they did not get the glory or Hollywood movie, but they were absolutely essential in helping win the war. (U.S. Army Transportation Corps 2023) Like Galatians 6:9, their quiet, consistent efforts bore a harvest others would reap. They didn't stop because of lack of recognition and because of that, the mission moved forward. Faithfulness and stamina in good works can help change the world.

WEEK 15 † REFUGE AND FORTRESS

Key Verse: *Psalm 91:1-2 (ESV)*

"He who dwells in the shelter of the Most High will abide in the shadow of the Almighty. I will say to the Lord, 'My refuge and my fortress, my God, in whom I trust."

Day 1

Mission Insight

Psalm 91 is a declaration of security in God Himself. The language of "shelter," "shadow," "refuge," and "fortress" is deeply familiar to those who served. You know the comfort of cover in combat zones and the anxiety of exposure outside the wire. This psalm does not deny danger it describes where to run when it comes. Trust in God is not a vague notion; it's a lived decision to abide in His presence, like taking cover under a shield that does not fail. In a world full of shifting threats, seen and unseen this promise remains; when you dwell in Him, you dwell in safety.

Personal Inspection

Where are feeling threatened, and is your body, heart, mind, and soul truly located in God's fortress?

Prayer

Lord, be my fortress today. Remind me that I can trust You to protect, cover, and keep me; even when I face dangers or life just feels uncertain, I shall know comfort in Your plan and protection.

Day 2

Mission Insight

Dwelling in the shelter of the Most High doesn't mean visiting God now and then. It means living in His presence 24/7 365 (no leap year doesn't give a day off). Veterans and service personnel understand the importance of being "in position" during a mission or at their assigned place of duty. Likewise spiritually, dwelling in God's shelter means showing up, day after day, in prayer, dependence, and trust doing good works under his protection.

Personal Inspection

Are you treating God's presence like a bunker or a fortress, an emergency shelter or a sturdy home?

Prayer

Father, I want to live with You, not just run to You in crisis. Teach me to dwell with you all of my days in your strength, not just visit when convenient or in need.

Day 3

Mission Insight

The "shadow of the Almighty" speaks of nearness. You can't be in someone's shadow unless you're close. For anyone of us who feels far from God this is an invitation. Get close, not by earning your way back, but by stepping back into His presence. The shadow is waiting to cover and be near you, He is ready to be your wingman along with being your King and Savior.

Personal Inspection
What would it look like to be courageous and move back under the shadow of God's protection today?

Prayer
Jesus, draw me near again. I do not want to be distant any longer, I want to walk in Your shadow.

Day 4

Mission Insight
Fortresses are built to withstand attack. That's who God is: strong, steady, unmoving. In combat, there's peace in knowing your position is fortified. Spiritually, God is your stronghold, not just emotionally, but eternally. He's not asking you to be the fortress, He already is and He cannot be toppled or overrun.

Personal Inspection
Where have you been trying to be your own fortress instead of leaning on God, are your walls being breached?

Prayer
Lord, I have been relying on my own walls. Break them down and let me take refuge in You alone for the fortress you provide is impenetrable and will stand eternally.

Day 5

Mission Insight

The psalm author (possibly Moses who wrote Psalm 90) declares, "My God, in whom I trust." Trust is personal. People often struggle with trust after betrayal, trauma, or disappointment, especially those like us because of the value we place on integrity and honor. But God is not like others. He is worthy of trust, not because life will be made easy, but because He is faithful through it all and will never leave you or forsake you.

Personal Inspection

What part of your heart is still hesitant to trust God and why, what leap of faith can you make?

Prayer

God, You know my fears and you know my history, all of it, help me trust again, beginning with YOU!

Day 6

Mission Insight

Dwelling in God's presence doesn't always change the battle, but it changes the fighter. Being covered by God gives you a different kind of confidence, perspective, peace, and security. You can step into hard situations with courage because you know you're not exposed rather you're sheltered by His power. The end result of what life has in store is unknown, what is awaiting us beyond it, we can be confident in.

Personal Inspection

What challenge are you facing right now that you need to approach under God's covering?

Prayer

Lord, go before me and be my 360 security all around me. Let Your presence change how I show up in every battle.

Day 7 After-Action Reflection

This week, we remembered that peace does not come from our strength, but from our shelter in Him. God is a refuge, a fortress, and a shadow that never shifts, He is the true strength. For combat veterans who know what it is like to rely on cover this should make sense, do not live exposed under enemy fire taking on the world foolishly by yourself and apart from God. Abide in His shelter, make His presence your permanent address. Trust Him always; not just when life falls apart, but every day with absolute faith.

Auxiliary Scriptures

- *Proverbs 18:10* "The name of the Lord is a strong tower; the righteous man runs into it and is safe."
- *Psalm 27:5* "He will hide me in His shelter in the day of trouble…"

Prayer

God, thank You that I don't have to be my own protection that You are my covering. Help me dwell in Your presence and trust in Your strength each day.

Field Note

The "Harlem Hellfighters" (named so by the Germans) of the 369th Infantry Regiment, an African American unit from New York, served more days in combat than any other American unit of its size in World War I. Fighting alongside French forces for 191 days straight, they endured the worst of combat with over 1400 casualties. Because of their skin color they were not permitted to be part of the farewell parade in 1918; however, their heroism and accomplishments became world renown. When they returned home on February 17, 1919, they were given a victory parade down New York's 5th Avenue and awarded the Croix de Guerre from the French Army. (National Museum of African American History & Culture, n.d.) The Harlem Hellfighters and the Soldier's Psalm (Psalm 91), shows us that with God we too will overcome and one day be welcomed home in victory!

WEEK 16 † CASTING YOUR CARES ON GOD

Key Verse: 1 *Peter 5:7 (ESV)*

"Casting all your anxieties on him, because he cares for you."

Day 1

Mission Insight
This short verse holds real power, written by the apostle Peter no stranger to fear, regret, and leadership pressure. It invites us to stop carrying what God never asked us to. You and I because of our service often become masters at compartmentalizing, stuffing down stress to focus on the mission, this trait often carries over to the civilian side of our lives. However, Peter gives us permission, a command, to release it. "Casting" means actively throwing something off, not gently laying it down. He does not tolerate your burdens rather He welcomes them purposely; because He truly cares, and you're not meant to do it all alone.

Personal Inspection
Where have you accepted you are always cared for, that God does for you because He truly loves you?

Prayer
Lord, I have been holding on to things I was never meant to carry. Teach me how to throw my worries onto You and rest in Your care.

Day 2

Mission Insight

Anxiety comes in many forms: fear of failure, worry about finances, guilt, thoughts about the future, things we have visited before. You may carry layers of unspoken stress never felt comfortable expressing. But this verse says "all your anxieties", not just the spiritual ones; every burden qualifies. God's care is wide enough for every worry, stop thinking you should not ask for help, He is waiting to answer your request.

Personal Inspection

What specific anxiety have you been keeping to yourself that God is ready to carry?

Prayer

Father, help me stop managing my anxiety in silence. You care so I must learn to trust You with it now.

Day 3

Mission Insight

Some people don't know what to do with your burden, news flash, God does. When you cast your anxieties on Him, they don't get ignored they get absorbed by Someone strong enough to carry them. Veterans trained to always "stay sharp" may feel weak asking for help but this verse redefines strength.

Personal Inspection

What does it look like for you to cast off and pray to God about your burdens?

Prayer
Jesus, I am tired of the recurrence of my fears in my life. Today I release them into Your hands, cast them off, and take up your yoke which is easy and burden light.

Day 4

Mission Insight
God's care is deeply personal. He's not just running the universe from afar, He's concerned about your next breath, your next appointment, your next sleepless night. Service members past and present often wrestle with whether anyone really sees or understands them. God does and He's not annoyed, put off, or despondent, He's attentive and engaged in your life.

Personal Inspection
Where in your life do you most need to feel God's nearness right now how are you open to it?

Prayer
God, remind me that I matter to You not just in the big picture, but in every small detail.

Day 5

Mission Insight
This verse follows a call to humility in verse 6. Why? Because casting your cares on God requires admitting you can't handle everything alone. Chances are you and I are used to being providers and protectors, and we may want to instinctually resist this, but the moment you honestly confess your limits, grace rushes in.

Personal Inspection

Is pride keeping you from casting your anxieties and what would surrender look like instead?

Prayer

Lord, break down my pride. I do not want to be self-sufficient in error I want to be grace dependent.

Day 6

Mission Insight

Anxiety multiplies in isolation. That's why this verse pairs so well with community. Casting your cares on God does not always happen alone it often starts by opening up to someone else, then praying together. God uses people to show His care, speaking to others and opening up can be a first step.

Personal Inspection

Who can you talk to this week to help lighten the burden you are carrying?

Prayer

Jesus, thank You for community, for those in my life who care. Give me courage to open up and find strength in Your body, the Church, and those close to me.

Day 7 After-Action Reflection

This week reminded us that God is not distant from our stress He without fail draws near to carry it. Casting your anxieties on Him is not weakness it is a superpower. It is trusting that the One who bled for you will not abandon you now. Those of us who have spent years holding everything in, be it service connected or not need this truth, you do not have to anymore, He cares for you. Period!

Auxiliary Scriptures

- *Matthew 6:34* "Do not be anxious about tomorrow..."
- *Philippians 4:6* "Do not be anxious about anything, but in everything... let your requests be made known to God."

Prayer

God, I cast my burdens, big and small onto You. I trust Your care, Your strength, and Your kindness. Thank You for being the One who carries me.

Field Note

Army Veteran Bryan Anderson, a Purple Heart recipient, lost both legs and his left hand to an IED in Iraq. Following his injury, Anderson battled depression and the overwhelming physical and emotional challenges of recovery. But rather than obsessing on the anxiety of his situation and what others may think about his limitations, he chose to focus on the positives and keep moving forward in life. In his memoir, "No Turning Back," Anderson describes how he learned to release his fears and burdens, and trust that his life still had purpose. (Mockenhaupt 2009) His journey reflects the heart of 1 Peter 5:7, casting anxiety on God, believe in the purpose and moving forward thriving in that peace.

WEEK 17 † TREASURE IN HEAVEN

Key Verse: *Matthew 6:19-21 (ESV)*

> **"Do not lay up for yourselves treasures on earth, where moth and rust destroy and where thieves break in and steal, but lay up for yourselves treasures in heaven... For where your treasure is, there your heart will be also."**

Day 1

Mission Insight

Jesus' words cut straight to the heart of our priorities. You may have sacrificed years in service, storing up tangible rewards like rank, medals, savings, or benefits. None of those are wrong, but Jesus reminds us they are temporary. Earthly treasures are fragile; heavenly treasures are eternal. The call is not to abandon responsibility but to prioritize investments that last forever: faith, relationships, and service to others. Where our treasure is, our heart will follow. If our treasure is Christ, our heart will never be lost.

Personal Inspection

What would God say that matters most to you, have you put your value in Him or things of this world?

Prayer

Lord, help me set my heart and priorities not on what fades away but rather what is of eternal value.

Day 2

Mission Insight

"Do not lay up… treasures on earth." Earthly wealth and accomplishments have expiration dates; we've all heard you cannot take it with you or if you have pockets take all you can take. Any of us who've lost things in life be it gear, rank or status know that nothing here is permanent. What lasts and what is of true value is what's done in love and obedience to God, that's your true legacy.

Personal Inspection

What's one "treasure" you have been holding too tightly that does not last and how has it compromised your priorities?

Prayer

Father, give me the wisdom beyond this world to value what lasts longer than this life and has real value.

Day 3

Mission Insight

"…where moth and rust destroy…" Jesus uses a very vivid imagery to remind us that decay is inevitable here for everything that is physical. Have you witnessed gear corrode, uniforms fade, and bases abandoned, then you certainly can relate; time and circumstance wear down everything, but the treasures in heaven are eternal and will forever be untarnished.

Personal Inspection

How can you shift more of your time, focus, and energy into eternal priorities and what are they?

Prayer

A simple but powerful prayer Lord; teach me to build what time can't destroy.

Day 4

Mission Insight

"Lay up… treasures in heaven." Logisticians and supply personnel know about stockpiling supplies. Jesus invites us to stockpile a different kind of resource; acts of faith, love, and service that God remembers forever. We don't and can't buy our way into heaven, through His grace and belief in Him we are assured. But we still are to do good works, and the rewards will meet us there.

Personal Inspection

What's one action you can take this week to add to your "heavenly account"?

Prayer

God, let my investments be eternal. Guide my body and heart to build for Your kingdom.

Day 5

Mission Insight

"…where thieves do not break in and steal." Security, safety, and force protection is a constant concern in military life, but there's no safer place for your treasures than heaven. No enemy can take them or destroy them. There is no greater safety or fortress than that which God provides.

Personal Inspection

How does knowing your spiritual treasures are secure affect your confidence today?

Prayer

Lord, thank You for the opportunity to do good works and that what I give to You is never lost.

Day 6

Mission Insight

"For where your treasure is, there your heart will be also." Your focus directs your life, how you live shows what you value. Living a lifestyle where everything is mission-focused you then know how objectives guide every choice. The same is true spiritually, your heart and subsequently your life follows what you truly treasure and is defined by its priorities. Jesus tells us to have a good heart, and to put your priorities and values in Him.

Personal Inspection

What does your current "treasure" reveal about your heart's direction? Unsure, ask yourself where does your money go and why?

Prayer

Jesus, align my heart with You and your teachings. Let my treasure be You and my actions reflect what I truly value.

Day 7 After-Action Reflection

This week reminds us that the safest, wisest investment is in God's kingdom. You know the value of protecting what is valuable but the greatest security is not in banks or bunkers, it is in Christ. Earthly treasures fade, but heavenly ones endure. When your treasure is in heaven, your heart will be anchored there too.

Auxiliary Scriptures

- *Luke 12:33–34* "Provide yourselves... a treasure in the heavens that does not fail."
- *1 Timothy 6:17–19* "Store up treasure... so that they may take hold of that which is truly life."

Prayer

Lord, You are my treasure. Secure my heart in You, and let my life reflect eternal values.

Field Note

Florence Nightingale, often called "The Lady with the Lamp," because of her night rounds checking the wounded; became world-famous for her service during the Crimean War (1853–1856). Born into a well to do British family, she was expected to enjoy a life of social privilege; instead, she felt called by God to serve the sick and suffering. Turning down comfort, wealth, and status, Nightingale traveled to the front line, where she organized field hospitals, dramatically improved sanitary conditions and reduced mortality rates among wounded soldiers. After the war, she continued advocating for public health reforms worldwide. (Selanders 2019) Nightingale's truly remarkable life embodied Matthew 6:19–21; she refused to store up earthly treasures, instead pouring her energy and resources into service that would leave a lasting legacy in both medicine and compassion.

WEEK 18 † ENDURANCE AND FOCUS ON CHRIST

Key Verse: *Hebrews 12:1-2 (ESV)*

"Surrounded by so great a cloud of witnesses...let us... lay aside every weight, and sin which clings so closely, and let us run with endurance the race that is set before us, looking to Jesus, the founder and perfecter of our faith, who for the joy that was set before him endured the cross..."

Day 1

Mission Insight

These verses paint the Christian life not as a stroll, but a race, a long one; filled with obstacles that we must overcome and leave behind us. I know you understand endurance whether from long physical fitness runs or long ruck marches, both are made easier by the less weight you carry. We are told to shed the extra weight: sin, burdens, distractions, shame, etc., and run our unique race with perseverance and eyes fixed on Jesus. He endured His suffering for our joy. Because of Him, we can keep going, while given the grace to lessen our burdens along the way.

Personal Inspection

When is the last time you inventoried what weighs you down, why have you not given that weight to God for him to lay aside for you?

Prayer
Jesus, help me run my race with endurance. Strip away what slows me down and keep my eyes locked on You as I traverse this world's terrain.

Day 2

Mission Insight
The "cloud of witnesses" refers to the faithful heroes of Hebrews 11: Abraham, Moses, Rahab, and others. You and me are not the first to feel tired or tested. You are not the first to run this race, God has given you this miracle of life for a purpose as He has others before you. We then should be students of history seeing those who have gone before us and set an example of how to run with eyes focused to God, let us draw strength and encouragement from their precedence.

Personal Inspection
Who has run their race well that inspires you or can inspire you to keep going?

Prayer
Lord, thank You for those who came before me showing me this race can be run. Let their faith and their example give me fuel for today's journey.

Day 3

Mission Insight
We carry more than we realize: guilt, expectations, fear, stress, grudges. These and other weights don't just slow us they sap us of positive energy, they are burdensome to our serving Gods purpose, and hence why He invites us to DROP THEM. God says its ok I got this and I got you; therefore, lay it down, then run free.

Personal Inspection
What unnecessary weight are you carrying like shackles that's keeping you from running well?

Prayer
God, show me what I need to release, what I carry needlessly. Help me let go and run lighter.

Day 4

Mission Insight
"Run the race set before us." Not someone else's race. Not your old identity. Not a version of you that no longer fits. God has a path tailored for you, today! Veterans sometimes struggle to find purpose or belonging post-service, or those currently serving struggle to find their purpose off the base; but this verse affirms you are still running your race; before you is still your life and your purpose that God has planned. Have faith!

Personal Inspection
How has your race changed and how can you embrace this next stretch with faith?

Prayer
Jesus, help me embrace where I am, and trust where You are leading me still with my purpose in mind that will serve Your glory not my own.

Day 5

Mission Insight
Looking to Jesus keeps us from drifting. There are plenty of distractions that take our focus way from Christ: pain, temptation, greed,

praise, resentment, selfishness, conformity, etc., but keeping our eyes on Christ grounds us. Jesus didn't just cheer from the sidelines, He took on the form of man, ran the hardest course and never quit; he is our first look and finest example of how we should be.

Personal Inspection

Where have your eyes drifted from Jesus and how can you refocus today?

Prayer

Lord, refocus my heart. When I am distracted, discouraged, or have the wrong priorities help me fix my eyes on You again.

Day 6

Mission Insight

Jesus endured the cross "for the joy set before Him." That joy was you, redeemed, restored, His as a gift from the Father. He saw the finish line and pressed through agony for love of you and me. Those who know service know what it's like to endure for others. Jesus calls us to endure now for the joy ahead just as he endured for us in his Joy.

Personal Inspection

As Jesus remained motivated despite his required sacrifice and suffering for the joy before him, what future joy is worth your present perseverance?

Prayer

God, give me vision to see beyond today and do not let this world distract or discourage me. Let your promise of eternal joy fuel my endurance.

Day 7 After-Action Reflection

This week, we've been called to run for Christ without burden. You're not running alone nor are you running without direction. Jesus ran the hardest race and now walks beside you in yours. Strip off the weight, unhobble yourself and let go of your burdens. Lock your eyes on the One who never looked away from you, in Him find inspiration to keep going even if one step at a time.

Auxiliary Scriptures

- *Philippians 3:13–14* "...forgetting what lies behind... I press on..."
- *Isaiah 40:29–31* "He gives power to the faint..."

Prayer

Lord, renew my strength. Help me run with endurance, with focus, and with joy. Thank You for going before me, lightening my burdens, and staying with me.

Field Note

U.S. Army Captain Gary M. Rose, a Special Forces combat medic, participated in Operation Tailwind in 1970 during the Vietnam War. For four grueling days behind enemy lines, Rose treated 60-70 wounded men under constant fire and even surviving one helicopter crash. Despite his own injuries he stayed with his team until the extraction was complete. Decades later in 2017, he was awarded the Medal of Honor. (Review of Captain Gary M. Rose 2018) His endurance and dedication to his purpose serves as an inspiration of what enduring through difficulty looks like. Like Hebrews 12, he ran the race set before him with perseverance, never abandoning the purpose he was put there to do.

WEEK 19 † OVERCOMING EVIL WITH GOOD

Key Verse: *Romans 12:21 (ESV)*

"Do not be overcome by evil, but overcome evil with good."

Day 1

Mission Insight

Paul's words cut against our instincts. When felt wronged, we want to react in-kind; when hurt, we want to hurt back. But this verse calls believers not to fight darkness with more darkness. Veterans of conflict have seen evil in forms many civilians never will. The temptation to harden your heart, to grow bitter or numb, is real, it is how we have coped. But Paul says evil wins when it changes us. The path forward is not to outfight the world rather it's to out-love it, meet injustice with integrity, replace hate with grace, and evil with good. This is not weakness its courage in taking the evil in this world head on and handing it defeat!

Personal Inspection

Where are you faced with evil and how are you reacting to it, with more evil or with good?

Prayer

Lord, when I feel overwhelmed by the darkness around or within me, teach me to fight with Your goodness, not my anger.

Day 2

Mission Insight

Evil is not just something that happened in a passage of scripture thousands of years ago, it's current and it is real. Many people often carry wounds from evil forced into or let into their lives. And with those wounds come choices: bitterness or healing, vengeance or grace. Goodness isn't pretending nothing happened, rather He says do not let evil define you, but rather overcome it, because you can with Him.

Personal Inspection

What pain are you carrying that threatens to turn into bitterness, how do you fight back with good?

Prayer

God, I do not want to be defined by what hurt me. Help me respond in a way that honors You and does not let evil win.

Day 3

Mission Insight

"Overcoming evil with good" does not always mean big battles. Sometimes it is refusing to gossip, choosing honesty, helping someone who wronged you. Every time you do good in the face of evil, you punch a hole in the darkness with the light the Holy Spirit has placed inside of you. We learned and know from our careers doing the little things right can have a big impact, same with small acts of kindness.

Personal Inspection

What is one small good choice you can make, an act of kindness, that can show evil has no hold on you?

Prayer
Lord, make me alert to the good I can do today, even if it feels small I know it matters.

Day 4

Mission Insight
Doing good means we can't ignore evil, however, we are to respond on God's terms, not ours. It means trusting that justice belongs to Him, and that his will be done; He will handle the punishments to be handed down. Warfighters trained for battle sometimes need to learn a new kind of strength away from the battlefield: that we don't have to right every wrong, but to do good, be the right example, and let God handle justice.

Personal Inspection
What would it look like to let God handle justice instead of feeling you must handle it yourself?

Prayer
Jesus, You are just. I release my need to control outcomes. Help me trust Your timing and character.

Day 5

Mission Insight
Goodness is an active surrender to God and chosen resistance to evil. When you refuse to return insult for insult or hate for hate, you're not weak, you're strong in Christ. Successful leaders know the strongest leaders keep calm, think clearly, and act with purpose. That's spiritual leadership too, the fight with evil is bigger than that moment, overcome the moment with good and win the war over evil.

Personal Inspection
How can your example of goodness influence someone else who is struggling?

Prayer
God, let my life reflect the kind of strength that honors You, not by demonstrating vengeance, but righteousness.

Day 6

Mission Insight
Overcoming evil with good is how the gospel works. Jesus didn't just teach this He lived it. He overcame betrayal, false accusations, torture, and death not with reprisal, but with mercy. Anyone with a bitter or jaded outlook who wonders if good can ever win need only look at the cross, the empty tomb, and victory over death and sin. Remember Jesus won, never forget that!

Personal Inspection
How does Christ's example shape how you deal with the injustices you've experienced?

Prayer
Lord, when I want to lash out, remind me of the cross. Teach me to follow Your way.

Day 7 After-Action Reflection

This week taught us that evil isn't just something we face, it is something we can overcome. But only with good. That good comes from God who gives us courage to forgive, strength to endure, and grace to heal. Experienced veterans don't need more hardness you are probably "crusty" enough already whether you know it or not. We need to choose to reflect Christ, not our pains or what's made us cynical. Evil has already lost; remember victory and the way has already been shown to you, so live like it!

Auxiliary Scriptures

- *Matthew 5:44* "Love your enemies and pray for those who persecute you."
- *Proverbs 25:21–22* "If your enemy is hungry, give him bread to eat..."

Prayer

Jesus, when I'm tempted to repay evil with more pain, remind me of who You are. Make me strong enough to be good and a reflection of you, even when it is difficult to turn the other cheek.

Field Note

Staff Sergeant Clinton Romesha received the Medal of Honor for his actions during the 2009 Battle of Kamdesh in Afghanistan, where a remote U.S. outpost was overrun by hundreds of Taliban fighters. Amid chaos and casualties, Romesha led counterattacks, directed air support, and repeatedly exposed himself to enemy fire to recover fallen soldiers. This brief description hardly does his actions justice. After the battle, he spoke not with hatred, but with humility, focused on the bravery of others and those who lost their lives. ("Medal of Honor Monday: Army Staff Sgt. Clint Romesha" 2025) His integrity under fire and his refusal to be hardened by the world's evils reflects Romans 12:21: he faced evil and responded with courage, sacrifice, and a goodness of heart.

WEEK 20 † PEACEMAKERS

Key Verse: *Matthew 5:9 (ESV)*

"Blessed are the peacemakers, for they shall be called sons of God."

Day 1

Mission Insight

This beatitude from Jesus maybe misunderstood as passive, it is not about avoiding conflict; but in the original Greek, "peacemaker" implies active work, as in to make it. It means stepping into chaos to restore what is broken. We brought up in the warrior mentality may bristle at the term "peace," having seen how fragile or arbitrary its political principals can be. Yet I am reminded Jesus did not call for peacekeepers He called for peacemakers, those who create space for reconciliation, truth, and bring healing in divided places. And when you take it on, Jesus says something remarkable, that you reflect your Father.

Personal Inspection

What would best define how you have lived, a peacekeeper or peacemaker?

Prayer

Lord, help me bring peace, not just hope for it. Use me as a force of healing in a world full of wounds.

Day 2

Mission Insight

Real peace sometimes follows real confrontation. Peacemakers do not ignore injustice, they enter those situations with courage and clarity, that the goal is peace and for reconciliation. Making peace can mean hard conversations, taking on adversity, forgiveness, or bridge-building; it is assuredly not easy but like many things with great reward, they are the hardest to do.

Personal Inspection

Where are you being called to pursue peace, even if it costs you time or comfort?

Prayer

God, make me bold enough to speak truth and kind enough to speak it with grace to bring peace in this world.

Day 3

Mission Insight

Being a peacemaker starts at home. Many of us or people we know, suffer from internal turmoil, and that can spill into relationships or work life. But Christ invites us to be people who calm storms (something he has some experience with) not create them. Peace in your home, marriage, or family does not happen by accident, it happens when you choose it daily and make the effort.

Personal Inspection

What relationship in your life needs you to step in as a peacemaker?

Prayer

Jesus, make me a vessel of Your peace, especially within me and with the people closest to me.

Day 4

Mission Insight

Making peace often means forgiving someone who does not deserve it. That's exactly what Christ did. We simply as humans sometimes struggle to let go of betrayal or disappointment, yet on the cross Jesus proclaimed forgiveness for those who put Him there. Remember when you forgive, you don't say, "What was done was okay." You say, "I won't let this wrong define me or my life."

Personal Inspection

Who do you need to forgive in order to find peace? Who do you need to forgive for yourself?

Prayer

Lord, I don't want to carry this anger any longer. Help me forgive as You forgave me though I wasn't worthy.

Day 5

Mission Insight

Jesus says peacemakers "shall be called sons of God." In the times the gospels were written, being called someone's son meant you carried their likeness. When you make peace, you bear the family resemblance of your Heavenly Father. Military past and present know about representing a unit or a service; however, this passage is about your representing the Kingdom and service to God.

Personal Inspection
How can you reflect God's character today through peacemaking internally or externally?

Prayer
Father, let my life show others what You are like. Help me reflect Your peace, even in tense moments.

Day 6

Mission Insight
Peacemaking doesn't mean peace will always come. Jesus Himself was rejected. But the calling isn't to produce results necessarily, it's to reflect God's heart. Whether others receive it or not, being a peacemaker makes you a witness to a different kind of kingdom, God's Kingdom.

Personal Inspection
Where have you been discouraged because peace hasn't come yet, and how can you remain faithful?

Prayer
Jesus, give me strength to keep making peace, even when it is hard. Let me leave the results to You.

Day 7 After-Action Reflection

This was one of my most enjoyable weeks to write I was reminded that peace is not passivity. It is action, rooted in the heart of God. We have all lived through conflict and know how fragile peace is, but that makes you uniquely equipped to help build it. Whether it's through forgiveness, advocacy, gentleness, or bold truth spoken in love, peacemaking matters. It echoes heaven and those who do it bear the title Jesus gives gladly, sons and daughters of God.

Auxiliary Scriptures

- *Romans 12:18* "If possible, so far as it depends on you, live peaceably with all."
- *2 Corinthians 5:18* "God... gave us the ministry of reconciliation."

Prayer

Lord, I want to be someone who makes peace wherever I go. Give me strength to confront, courage to forgive, and love to bring people together. Let my life reflect Yours.

Field Note

General George C. Marshall, Army Chief of Staff during WWII and later, Secretary of State, helped lead not only in war but in peace. Post-war, he spearheaded the Marshall Plan, which brought economic recovery and reconciliation to war-ravaged Europe. Instead of seeking revenge or dominance, Marshall sought healing. In 1953, he received the Nobel Peace Prize, not for avoiding conflict, but for pursuing restoration. (Healy, n.d.) His legacy as a peacemaker echoes Matthew 5:9: blessed are those who rebuild, who reconcile, who reflect the heart of God in a broken world.

WEEK 21 † SHARPENING ONE ANOTHER

Key Verse: *Proverbs 27:17 (ESV)*

"Iron sharpens iron, and one man sharpens another."

Day 1

Mission Insight

This short proverb captures a prevailing truth, we are shaped through relationship. For those like us this is intuitive, units are forged through shared hardship, mutual respect, and accountability. "Iron sharpens iron" is not gentle, it implies friction, shaping, and strength gained through adversity. In the spiritual life, we grow stronger when we surround ourselves with those who speak truth, walk with integrity, and push us toward Christ. Isolation and avoidance dull the edge, but fellowship, Christ-centered relationships, and shared adversity taking the hard rights over the easy wrongs makes us sharper for the battles ahead.

Personal Inspection

What way does the iron that you are, shape others, are you sharpening others in Christ or something else?

Prayer

God, bring people into my life who make me better, who sharpen my faith, challenge my heart, and help me reflect You more clearly.

Day 2

Mission Insight

Sharpening only happens through contact. That means getting close and being vulnerable. Veterans more so than those still serving are often slow to trust, used to relying on themselves in post service life more than the average Joe. But spiritual sharpening cannot happen in isolation. Growth comes through friendship, brotherhood, accountability, and even being challenged. In service and out of service preserve and seek this type of growth in your life.

Personal Inspection

Who in your life sharpens you and are you letting them close enough to do it?

Prayer

Lord, help me let down my guard with the people You've placed in my life. Use them to help me grow.

Day 3

Mission Insight

Sharpening isn't always comfortable. Sometimes it means enduring: constructive criticism, being corrected, truth-telling, or being challenged. But the goal of sharpening is clarity, dedication to the Gospel's teachings, and serving our purpose. As any of us who have ever wielded a knife or blade know that dull tools can be dangerous or counterproductive. In God's hands be that sharpened piece of iron, a useful tool, in the service of doing His will in this life.

Personal Inspection

When was the last time someone challenged you in a way that helped you grow?

Prayer

Father, give me humility to receive sharpening even when it stings. Help me become more effective for Your purposes.

Day 4

Mission Insight

You don't just need sharpening you're called to sharpen others. That doesn't mean being critical or harsh. It means loving people enough to speak truth, offer encouragement, and walk with them toward growth. Those with military experience often lead by example, so let your example point people to Christ.

Personal Inspection

Who in your life could benefit from your wisdom, challenge, or encouragement right now?

Prayer

God, make me a source of strength and refinement for someone else. Use my words and example to sharpen others so they too can be a useful tool to do good works in their lives as well.

Day 5

Mission Insight

Sharpening requires consistency. You don't hone a blade with one pass of the file or turn on the grinding stone, you do it over time. In Christian community, we need regular connection with people who help us stay sharp. Weekly check-ins, prayer partners, or small groups are part of God's design for ongoing refinement.

Personal Inspection

What's one step you can take to build regular, sharpening relationships in your life?

Prayer

Lord, give me the discipline to stay connected, not just when it's easy or just in the hard times, but let me be consistent in my faith and communion with others to keep me sharp in the word.

Day 6

Mission Insight

There's a reason this verse uses iron, not wood or clay though all can be shaped. Iron speaks of strength, resilience, and enduring impact. Experienced veterans know the value of strong people in hard places. Surround yourself with those whose character is tested, whose walk is real, and whose faith challenges yours.

Personal Inspection

What kind of people are you surrounding yourself with and are they making you stronger in your walk with Christ?

Prayer

Jesus, help me choose friends who sharpen me and make me the kind of friend who sharpens others.

Day 7 After-Action Reflection

This week reminded us that strength is never in being alone. Just as iron sharpens iron, God uses people to shape people. In the military, lives depend on trust, teamwork, and accountability. The same is true in the body of Christ. Do not isolate yourself and do not fear the friction. Welcome the sharpening that leads to spiritual edge and purpose. Remember you're not just being sharpened you are helping someone else get ready for the fight as well.

Auxiliary Scriptures

- *Ecclesiastes 4:9–10* "Two are better than one… if either fall, one can lift the other."
- *Hebrews 10:24–25* "Stir one another up to love and good works…"

Prayer

Lord, thank You for the people who have sharpened me. Teach me to be both teachable and a teacher. Help me stay sharp and help others do the same.

Field Note

Command Sergeant Major Bennie G. Adkins served three tours in Vietnam and was awarded the Medal of Honor for his actions during a 1966 battle at A Shau where he rescued wounded comrades, and evaded capture for 48 hours. However, that was not all that defined his service and taught at the jungle school from lessons he learned in Vietnam. He went on to be a teacher for 10 years and separately mentored young Soldiers or those interested in joining the military. (Review of COMMAND SGT. MAJ. BENNIE G. ADKINS 2010) He didn't just survive or do for himself, he sharpened others with wisdom, assistance, and encouragement. Like Proverbs 27:17, his legacy lives on not just by actions on the battlefield but through ones he shaped during and after service.

WEEK 22 † SEASONS AND TIMING

Key Verse: *Ecclesiastes 3:1 (ESV)*

"For everything there is a season, and a time for every matter under heaven."

Day 1

Mission Insight

A poetic and profound verse in Scripture on the rhythms of life. We are no strangers to seasons: deployment, training, returning home, transition, retirement. Each season carries its own challenges and blessings. Ecclesiastes reminds us, life is not meant to stay static. There are times for action and times for stillness, for building and breaking down, for mourning and dancing. The key isn't controlling the seasons it's learning to move with them, trusting that God oversees them all. Accept and live in the time you're in, while trusting the One who holds time itself.

Personal Inspection

Does knowing the seasons are always changing make you realize your need for God's consistency?

Prayer

Lord, help me discern the season I am in and trust You through its changes. Teach me to move with You, rely on your steadfastness, and not resist You.

Day 2

Mission Insight

Those from the Army to the Space Force and every branch in-between often struggle with transition. I know I have in my career, the shift from structure to flexibility, from intensity to stillness. But this verse affirms that each part of life has its own time and reason even if God's plan may be beyond comprehension at that time. You're not behind, you're not ahead, you're in a season as God planned and He is in it with you.

Personal Inspection

What season are you in right now and how is God inviting you to respond to it?

Prayer

Father, give me peace about the phase I am in. Let me walk through it with trust, not frustration.

Day 3

Mission Insight

Sometimes we try to hold onto old seasons because they felt purposeful. Veterans may long for the clarity of mission, felt purpose, and camaraderie. But God has new purposes for new times. Wisdom means letting go of what was, so you can embrace what is and journey to what's ahead.

Personal Inspection

Is there a past season you are clinging to instead of stepping fully into the present?

Prayer
God, help me release the old chapter with gratitude and step into this one with courage.

Day 4

Mission Insight
Every season has a reason. Even the painful ones. Grief, loss, waiting… they're not wasted. God uses them to shape, refine, and prepare us. You may not see the purpose now, but Ecclesiastes reminds you: there is one.

Personal Inspection
What difficult season in your past eventually revealed God's purpose how can you use that experience to help you trust in God now?

Prayer
Jesus, thank You that nothing in my life is random. Use even the hard times to draw me closer to You and advance me in the purpose you have for me.

Day 5

Mission Insight
This verse invites patience. In a culture that rushes, God reminds us that fruit takes time. You can't rush healing, growth, or calling. You and I with that military mindset often want to "just get on with it," but some seasons are about learning to be still and trust.

Personal Inspection
What area of your life do you need to stop rushing, take a tactical pause, and start trusting?

Prayer
Lord, slow me down, help me trust Your timing, even when I do not understand it.

Day 6

Mission Insight
There is assurance and freedom in knowing not every season is forever. If you're in a season of grief, doubt, or confusion, know it won't last. God will move us forward. His mercies are new with every sunrise, and His grace carries us into the next chapter, trust and keep walking forward with Him.

Personal Inspection
What hard season do you need hope to endure right now? See and envision how God will get you through it.

Prayer
Father, remind daily and as I need that this season will pass and You will sustain me through it.

Day 7 After-Action Reflection

This week reminded us that life moves in seasons. You may be in a time of rebuilding, grieving, resting, or rediscovering purpose. Wherever you are, God is already there, do not fight the season. Learn from it, lean into it and Trust that He wastes nothing not even the confusing chapters. His timing is perfect, and His presence is faithful in every moment under heaven.

Auxiliary Scriptures

- *Galatians 6:9* "In due season we will reap, if we do not give up."
- *Psalm 31:15* "My times are in Your hand..."

Prayer

God, thank You that every part of my life is seen by You. Help me live with wisdom, patience, and faith no matter what season I am in.

Field Note

Colonel Gail Halvorsen, known as the "Berlin Candy Bomber" served during the Berlin Airlift in 1948–1949. Amid postwar tension and volatility, he noticed the emotional toll on German children. In a season of rebuilding and hardship, he began dropping candy from his aircraft (Operations Little Vittles) with handkerchief parachutes. His simple act of kindness sparked international goodwill and earned him the affection of many. ("Gail Halvorsen | American Experience | PBS," n.d.) Halvorsen discerned the moment he was in, and acted accordingly, dropping over 250,000 parachutes. As Ecclesiastes 3:1 teaches, knowing the season helps us serve faithfully within it.

WEEK 23 † CREATED ANEW

Key Verse: *2 Corinthians 5:17 (ESV)*

"Therefore, if anyone is in Christ, he is a new creation. The old has passed away; behold, the new has come."

Day 1

Mission Insight

This verse is not a metaphor; it is truly a spiritual reality. Paul proclaims that when we place our faith in Christ, something irreversible happens, WE ARE MADE NEW. For veterans and service members, this is a powerful promise, no matter what we were for however long, the gospel says that identity is not final. In Christ, your story doesn't end in brokenness or however He found you. The old is not ignored, it is transformed, a new chapter has begun. You are not who you were, you're better, you're NEW and you will continue to be who God is forming you to be.

Personal Inspection

When in your day do you remind yourself, that through faith you are new and forever redeemed?

Prayer

Jesus, thank You that my past does not define me. Make me new each day as I walk with You.

Day 2

Mission Insight

Becoming a new creation doesn't mean forgetting your past it means your past no longer has the final word or hold over you anymore. For example many veterans often struggle to reconcile who they were in uniform with who they are now. In Christ, you are both redeemed and repurposed, it is never too late for him to do both in your life. Remember nothing is wasted, as we learned in Week 22.

Personal Inspection

What part of your past do you need to stop letting define your present?

Prayer

God, help me believe that I am more than my memories. Let my new life in You, lead the way!

Day 3

Mission Insight

New creation means new thinking, new believing; Christ reshapes the inside, your spirit, your heart. Those of us used to being on high alert, cynicism, or emotional numbness, can be renewed from the inside out, leaving that way of being behind. This isn't self-help, it's spiritual resurrection by a power and love that can only come through Jesus Christ.

Personal Inspection

What mindset have you been stuck in that Jesus wants to transform, will you let Him?

Prayer

Lord, change not just my circumstances change my mind. Make my thoughts new and rooted in truth inspired not by the world I live in but by your Kingdom and the Holy Spirit.

Day 4

Mission Insight

Being a new creation can be a process, old ways might not disappear overnight, but know transformation is happening and your heart has changed when you surrender to Christ. Those of us trained to track progress can take heart: your transformation is ongoing. God's grace is not permission to stay the same, it's power to grow, change, and be in Him as you were meant to be.

Personal Inspection

Where have you expected instant change and how can you instead lean into long-term transformation?

Prayer

Jesus, thank You for walking with me at the pace of grace, help me keep moving forward, even when growth feels slow.

Day 5

Mission Insight

This verse is for anyone, no exceptions. That includes the combat vet with regrets, the spouse with guilt, the leader who stumbled, or the ones incarcerated. You are not disqualified! He makes something entirely new, he is not limited by the past, the current conditions, he is all places and can meet you where you are, any place any time.

Personal Inspection
What lie about your worth or future needs to be silenced by this truth?

Prayer
God, let Your voice speak louder than my shame. Remind me that I belong to You and You make all things new no matter the current condition.

Day 6

Mission Insight
A new creation has a new purpose your mission may look different now, but it's no less meaningful. We may sometimes wonder daily, "What now?", I have asked this very question. The answer is in the verse just after this one: you are now an ambassador for Christ. You have a new assignment that all else in your life will follow after, live for Him first and all else will work out.

Personal Inspection
What does it mean for you to live like someone with a new mission in Christ?

Prayer
Jesus, show me what You have placed in front of me. Help me live each day like I'm on Kingdom orders.

Day 7 After-Action Reflection

This week reminded us that in Christ, the old has passed and the new has come. You are not your past. You are not your failures. You are not even your best moments. You are new. That is the promise and the power of the gospel. Veterans who wonder if it is too late to change need this truth, if you are a believer than you already have the answer that it's never too late, because Christ lives in you!

Auxiliary Scriptures

- *Romans 6:4* "We were buried… in order that… we too might walk in newness of life."
- *Ezekiel 36:26* "I will give you a new heart and put a new spirit within you."

Prayer

Jesus, thank You for making me new. Remind me daily that I am not defined by what was, but by what You are doing in me now and my belief and surrender to You.

Field Note

Sergeant Noah Galloway, a double amputee from the Iraq War, was forced to have to reinvent himself from an Infantry Soldier into something new. Through resiliency, drive, and physical fitness he not only became a new man but excelled, living by the mantra of "No Excuses." He reclaimed purpose and used his story to inspire others. Galloway became a motivational speaker, mental health advocate, and Author writing a book titled, "Living with No Excuses; the Remarkable Rebirth of an American Soldier." (Galloway 2019) His life embodies the message of 2 Corinthians 5:17: the old has gone, the new has come. Brokenness didn't disqualify him; it became the platform for transformation.

WEEK 24 † GOD'S PRESENCE

Key Verse: *Psalm 23:4 (ESV)*

"Even though I walk through the valley of the shadow of death, I will fear no evil, for you are with me; your rod and your staff, they comfort me."

Day 1

Mission Insight

Psalm 23 is a beloved passage for good reason and even dares to speak to the darkest places of human experience. The "valley of the shadow of death" is personal for anyone who has faced true loss or threat. Active military and retired know what it is like to walk through danger, fear, or profound risk. But this verse declares something resolute, that we do not walk alone. God's presence is not reserved for the mountain top, it shines bright even in the valley. His rod and staff, a symbol of protection and guidance, remind us that even in the most uncertain terrain or distant lands, we are not abandoned.

Personal Inspection

What does walking through the valley look like to you… now how does it change when you picture Christ there walking along beside you?

Prayer
Lord, I do not want to walk through this valley, but I thank You that I do not walk it alone. Be my comfort and guide in the dark.

Day 2

Mission Insight
Fear thrives in the shadows when the path is unclear, and the threats feel close. But David says, "I will fear no evil." Not because he's fearless, but because God is near. Any of us who've served in dangerous places or circumstances can appreciate the feeling when support is nearby, presence changes everything. And God's presence never leaves.

Personal Inspection
What fear are you facing right now and how can God's presence bring comfort in it?

Prayer
God, my fear is real, but You are greater. Help me remember that You go with me, even here.

Day 3

Mission Insight
The valley is not the destination it's the path through. You're not stuck here forever nor does God want you to be. The Shepherd leads us through dark places, not into dead ends. Any soul dealing with grief, depression, or trauma can adhere to this, the valley is real, but it's not the end.

Personal Inspection
What valley are you walking through and how can you trust that it's not permanent?

Prayer
Lord, remind me that this is a passage, not a prison. Lead me through it with steady steps.

Day 4

Mission Insight
"Your rod and your staff, they comfort me." The rod defends, the staff guides. Like me I am sure you appreciate good leadership especially under pressure. God is both warrior and shepherd. He protects us from evil and leads us when we can't see the way, just like a good leader would do.

Personal Inspection
How is God's leadership comforting you or where do you need to let Him take the lead?

Prayer
Jesus, You are strong, gentle, and every present. Let me trust Your hand to both guide and defend me today.

Day 5

Mission Insight
This verse doesn't promise the absence of evil but it does promise victory over fear. For those who've served, fear can be connected to any number of things. But God doesn't shame us for being afraid.

He draws near to give us courage not from within ourselves, but from His nearness.

Personal Inspection
What fear have you been trying to fight alone and how can you give it to God?

Prayer
God, I don't want to carry this fear anymore. Be bigger than the darkness in front of me let me feel the courage that comes with knowing you fight this fear with me.

Day 6

Mission Insight
Sometimes the greatest comfort isn't a change in circumstance it's knowing we're not alone. That's the heart of this verse. Whether in combat, hospitals, therapy sessions, or silent nights, God's presence is the difference between despair and hope, uncertainty, and confidence.

Personal Inspection
When was a time you felt God's presence in a difficult moment do you know he can be there in all moments to matter how big or small?

Prayer
Lord, help me feel Your nearness again. Remind me that You are closer than my fears.

Day 7 After-Action Reflection

This week has been a reminder that valleys are part of the journey but they're not walked alone. If you've faced darkness, danger, or deep emotional struggle, Psalm 23:4 offers hope, God is with you. He defends, guides, and comforts. His presence doesn't remove every threat, but it does remove the power of fear to control, keep walking, the Shepherd clears the way ahead.

Auxiliary Scriptures

- *Isaiah 43:2* "When you pass through the waters, I will be with you..."
- *Romans 8:38–39* "Nothing can separate us from the love of God..."

Prayer

Jesus, walk with me through every valley. Help me trust that You are near, even when I feel alone. Comfort me with Your strength, and guide me with Your love.

Field Note

Lieutenant Colonel Charles W. "Chuck" Kettles, an Army helicopter pilot in Vietnam, earned the Medal of Honor for his heroic actions during a 1967 mission in Duc Pho. Under intense enemy fire, Kettles repeatedly flew into danger to evacuate wounded soldiers. After several trips, he learned that eight men had been left behind. Without hesitation and without cover or support he returned alone, rescuing the last eight Soldiers. ("Lt. Col. Charles Kettles | Medal of Honor Recipient | U.S. Army" 2016) In the valley of the shadow of death, his courage was a vessel of comfort and rescue. Psalm 23:4 and LTC Kettles' example illustrates how Jesus walks into the valley with us, His leadership and courage bring us comfort.

WEEK 25 † CONFESSION AND FORGIVENESS

Key Verse: *1 John 1:9 (ESV)*

"If we confess our sins, he is faithful and just to forgive us our sins and to cleanse us from all unrighteousness."

Day 1

Mission Insight

This verse is a lifeline for anyone burdened by guilt. You may wrestle with moral injury, the invisible weight of leadership decisions made under pressure, things witnessed, or mistakes. But here, John delivers gospel clarity confession is not about judgement it's about freedom. God is not reluctant to forgive He is *faithful* to do so. When we come honestly and repentant in heart, He forgives and cleanses. The shame, the stain, all washed away in grace. You do not have to earn it you just have to bring it.

Personal Inspection

What can God see in your heart that you are truly sorrowful for, he forgives, so why still carry it?

Prayer

Lord, I confess what I have tried to hide. Thank You for meeting me not with judgment, but with mercy.

Day 2

Mission Insight
Confession is not for God's sake He already knows; It is for ours. It takes the weight off our chest and brings hidden things into the healing light. Warriors are often conditioned to "suck it up," but spiritual strength comes through surrender, not suppression, expression not silence.

Personal Inspection
What burden have you been silently carrying that you need to bring to God to let him forgive?

Prayer
God, I've kept this inside long enough. I give it to You now trusting You to meet me with grace.

Day 3

Mission Insight
Forgiveness isn't based on how bad the sin was it is based on how faithful God is. Some veterans feel their past disqualifies them from full restoration. But the verse says, He is faithful and just. Forgiveness is not a loophole. It's a promise kept by a God for those truly repentant of heart.

Personal Inspection
What lie have you believed about your sin being too big for God's forgiveness?

Prayer
Jesus, thank You that my worst mistakes do not surprise You. Help me live in the freedom of being truly forgiven.

Day 4

Mission Insight
Confession doesn't just address what we've done it begins to restore who we are. Cleansing is about more than wiping a record clean it's about healing identity. Those who feel "dirty" from what they've seen or done need to hear this: God doesn't just erase sin He restores souls.

Personal Inspection
Where do you need God to not only forgive but *cleanse*?

Prayer
Lord, I do not just want pardon I want restoration. Wash the stain, not just the record as only you can do.

Day 5

Mission Insight
Shame isolates. It says, "You're the only one." But confession brings us back into community with God and with others. Those suffering in silence often feel uniquely broken but Scripture says otherwise; all fall short, and all are invited back through grace.

Personal Inspection
How might confession actually reconnect you rather than isolate you?

Prayer
God, bring me back from hiding. Let Your forgiveness draw me into honest community with You and lighten my path back to being part of Your Kingdom.

Day 6

Mission Insight

Some people think confession is just a one-time act. But it is a daily rhythm of our spiritual health. Just like personal hygiene, we need soul-cleansing daily. Routine and discipline are familiar strengths, setting a routine and being disciplined about our spiritual rhythm means actively and daily acknowledging our sins sincerely and be quick to confess, quick to walk clean.

Personal Inspection

How can confession become part of your daily spiritual rhythm, not just a crisis reaction?

Prayer

Jesus, keep me honest and humble. Let me come to You quickly and often, trusting Your mercy every day for you know my heart.

Day 7 After-Action Reflection

This week, we have been reminded that confession isn't defeat, it is deliverance. God does not forgive reluctantly He does it faithfully, because that's who He is. Everyone needs this truth, no matter how deep the stain, grace goes deeper. You are not beyond cleansing. You are not beyond welcome. Confess. Receive. Walk free.

Auxiliary Scriptures

- *Psalm 32:5* "I acknowledged my sin… and you forgave the iniquity…"
- *Isaiah 1:18* "Though your sins are like scarlet, they shall be white as snow…"

Prayer

Jesus, thank You for forgiveness I could not earn but is made possible by sacrificing yourself on the cross. Cleanse me, restore me, and help me live like someone who has been made new.

Field Note

John Newton, who penned the poem and later hymn "Amazing Grace" was an 18th-century British sailor and slave ship captain. Newton lived a life marked by lack of moral self-control, discipline, and participation in the brutal transatlantic slave trade. But during a violent storm at sea in the 1740s, he cried out to God for saving, marking the beginning of his conversion. In the years that followed, Newton eventually became an ordained minister and helped inspire the abolition of slavery in England. ("The Creation of 'Amazing Grace' | Articles and Essays | Amazing Grace | Digital Collections | Library of Congress" 2015) His life epitomizes 1 John 1:9; confession met by God's faithfulness and forgiveness, can lead to amazing transformation and service.

WEEK 26 † GOD'S PLANS AND HOPE

Key Verse: *Jeremiah 29:11 (ESV)*

"For I know the plans I have for you, declares the Lord, plans for welfare and not for evil, to give you a future and a hope."

Day 1

Mission Insight

This is one of the most quoted promises in the Bible, but its power grows when we remember the context, God gave it to people in exile. Relevant today to those who are displaced, discouraged, and far from where they wanted to be. Many of us may know or have known that feeling; uncertain of the next step, burdened by the past, unsure of their future. But here God speaks plainly saying I still have a plan for you. God sees beyond the self-imposed exile, He sees the comeback, the homecoming. Hope isn't hype it's rooted in God's character and commitment to your story and your future.

Personal Inspection

What lenses do you use to look forward, is it through God's eyes or eyes with a different priority?

Prayer

Lord, when I cannot see the way forward, help me trust that You already have a plan. Anchor my hope in You.

Day 2

Mission Insight

God's plans are not always our plans and that's often the hardest part. If you're used to making things happen which you probably are, then you may struggle when life seems out of control. But God doesn't promise easy He promises purpose. His plans are always for good, even when they take us through detours or weren't necessarily our idea.

Personal Inspection

Where have you been disappointed that God's plans didn't match your own and how might He be leading you anyway?

Prayer

Father, help me trust You even when I don't understand. Your plans are better than mine.

Day 3

Mission Insight

The people who first heard this verse were still in exile. The promise wasn't immediate the time in the wilderness was long but it was certain. Hope doesn't erase present struggle, it gives you strength inside it. If we find ourselves in a season of recovery or transition it may feel like the breakthrough is far off, but don't ever forget God is still working, He is always working, and His plan is certain.

Personal Inspection

What would it look like to hope with endurance even while you wait for Gods plan to develop?

Prayer
God, help me believe that You're working behind the scenes. Let hope rise in me even when I don't feel it yet.

Day 4

Mission Insight
"Plans for welfare" doesn't mean material success it means peace, completeness, restoration. Veterans seeking purpose after military service often want clarity of future. Soldiers coming up on a new duty assignment want assurance of what, when, and where. Yet God offers more, He offers wholeness; He wants you healed, whole, and walking in peace, all else will work out, if you trust in God's plan first.

Personal Inspection
What part of your life still feels fractured and how might God be working to restore it?

Prayer
Jesus, I need more than direction I need healing as I move forward. Thank You for working to make me whole, let me be open to Your ways.

Day 5

Mission Insight
When you've faced loss, injury, trauma, or have anxiety the future can feel like a threat instead of a promise. But this verse reminds us that God holds what's ahead. You don't have to live backward or stuck in the past. In Christ, there is still something good in front of you something worth walking toward.

Personal Inspection

What fear about the future do you need to release into God's hands how can you give Him control?

Prayer

Lord, I release my anxiety about what's next. I trust that You continue to walk ahead of me.

Day 6

Mission Insight

God's plan isn't just personal it's communal. Jeremiah told the people to seek peace for the city they were in. Be it veterans who are out or service members who are in we can sometimes feel isolated, but God's hope often shows up through community, service, and shared mission even in seasons or places you didn't choose or expect.

Personal Inspection

Where might God be calling you to serve or plant hope even if life hasn't gone according to plan?

Prayer

Father, use me in this season. Don't let me wait for perfect conditions let me plant hope where I find myself now.

Day 7 After-Action Reflection

Jeremiah 29:11 is not simply a motivational quote it's a pledge. God's people were in a place they did not want to be, and He still said "I've got plans for you." Maybe you are in a chapter you would not have written but you are not off course. God's hand is still on you, hope is still alive and the future is still full of promise. Not because life is predictable, but because God is faithful.

Auxiliary Scriptures

- *Romans 8:28* "All things work together for good..."
- *Proverbs 3:5–6* "Trust in the Lord with all your heart..."

Prayer

God, thank You that You never lose sight of my future, even when I do. Let Your plans guide me, and let Your hope sustain me.

Field Note

Captain Scott Smiley, an Army Ranger and West Point graduate, was blinded by a suicide bomber in Iraq in 2005. He could have let that moment end his story, but instead he chose to trust that God still had a plan. He went on to become the U.S. Army's first blind active-duty officer, earned an MBA, taught at West Point, and even climbed Mt. Ranier. Through faith, resilience, and support, he embraced a new future. (Veterans Airlift 2007) His journey reflects Jeremiah 29:11: even when life breaks your vision, God's vision for your life remains full of purpose and hope.

WEEK 27 † SPIRITUAL ARMOR

Key Verse: *Ephesians 6:11 (ESV)*

"Put on the whole armor of God, that you may be able to stand against the schemes of the devil."

Day 1

Mission Insight

Paul uses vivid military imagery to describe the Christian life not as a stroll, but a fight. All warfighters understand the importance of armor, protective gear, tactical preparation, and readiness. In Ephesians, Paul describes a different kind of armor: truth, righteousness, peace, faith, salvation, and the Word of God. This armor is not issued from a supply line it is forged through faith and worn daily. Spiritual warfare is real, and so are the enemy's tactics of deception, division, discouragement. But we are not left unprotected, in Christ we are equipped to be victorious.

Personal Inspection

What of truth, righteousness, peace, faith, salvation, and the Word of God is missing from your kit, where are you vulnerable and unprotected?

Prayer

Lord, help me take up Your armor today. I do not want to fight unprotected clothe me in what I need to stand strong against the evils in this world.

Day 2

Mission Insight

Armor does not help if it is not worn. Paul says, put it on! That is a daily intentional choice we need to make, to suit up! Put in harm's way we know the danger of complacency, of skipping checks or getting too comfortable; it is when bad things usually happen. Spiritually, we are called to be alert, prepared, and equipped, not fearful, but ready and confident.

Personal Inspection

What piece of spiritual armor have you been neglecting and how can you put it on again today?

Prayer

God, wake me up to the battle I am in. Help me dress in Your truth, not my own strength.

Day 3

Mission Insight

The "schemes of the devil" are not usually dramatic they are subtle like lies whispered into the soul, doubt, isolation and division. Any of us who have experience dealing with shame, anger, or addiction know these tactics firsthand. But armor protects it absorbs impacts. it keeps you standing when the hits come, and can even delivery you from evil.

Personal Inspection

What lie or doubt have you been believing that God's armor can protect you from?

Prayer
Lord, speak truth into the places where I have been deceived. Protect me from all evils around me, help me stand firm in You.

Day 4

Mission Insight
This armor isn't decorative, it's functional. Truth stabilizes, righteousness guards, peace steadies your steps, faith extinguishes fear, and salvation secures eternity. Scripture is your manual and the Holy Spirit your weapon. We once carried gear to fight earthly battles, now still warriors, we fight with divine tools.

Personal Inspection
Which piece of God's armor do you most need in this season and why, are you wearing it?

Prayer
Jesus, thank You for providing everything I need to stand. Strengthen what is weak and sharpen what is dull so that I am better prepared for the daily spiritual battle.

Day 5

Mission Insight
Paul does not say, win the war, he says, "stand". Jesus has already secured victory over the world the war is won. However battles still rage on, our job is to remain grounded, geared up, and faithful while continuing the fight against evil until the day He returns.

Personal Inspection
Where do you need to stop and stand strong in God's armor that He has already given you?

Prayer
God, grant me the courage to be convicted and confident in this battle for good, teach me the power of standing firm in Your strength and being bold in my faith.

Day 6

Mission Insight
The armor of God is not issued to individuals alone it's for all who are willing to put it on. Soldiers fight best when they have the resources and numbers; Spiritually this is no different, we need each other. Armor up but do not go it alone, join other in faith during this fight there is power in numbers.

Personal Inspection
Who is standing beside you in your spiritual battles and who needs you beside them?

Prayer
Father, make me a faithful battle buddy to someone else. Help me fight well as part of Your army, not of one to conquer land but to liberate souls on our march to your Kingdom.

Day 7 After-Action Reflection

This week reminded us that the Christian life is not always safe but it is secure. We are not left defenseless, we have been given armor forged in heaven and tested on earth, the enemy is real but so is our victory in Christ. Veterans of all stripes who know the weight of gear can take comfort that the armor of God is light on the soul, but indestructible in battle. Wear it daily!

Auxiliary Scriptures

- *2 Corinthians 10:4* "The weapons of our warfare are not of the flesh…"
- *1 Thessalonians 5:8* "…put on the breastplate of faith and love…"

Prayer

Jesus, thank You for giving me what I need to stand. Help me wear Your armor with confidence and trust Your strength in every battle I face.

Field Note

Lieutenant Colonel Dave Grossman, U.S. Army, military psychologist and man of faith has spent his post-military career training soldiers and civilians in how to deal with the stress of combat and other violent or stressful situations. He speaks and writes about the importance of preserving with the right tools, skills, and proper mindset that he calls "The Bulletproof Mind." Grossman encourages warriors to protect their minds, not just their bodies in combat. (Grossman on Truth 2024) His insights echo Ephesians 6:11; in a world of invisible battles, God's armor isn't optional, it's essential. Those who suit up with faith, truth, and righteousness are those who endure.

WEEK 28 † NO CONDEMNATION

Key Verse: *Romans 8:1 (ESV)*

"There is therefore now no condemnation for those who are in Christ Jesus."

Day 1

Mission Insight

This verse marks a turning point in Paul's letter to the Romans, a bold declaration of freedom. After describing the struggle with the old ways in chapter 7, Paul opens chapter 8 with a verdict that Christians don't have to follow the Old Testament laws. For those currently serving, there is a message here for you, don't wait till the end of your career to commit to Christ, make him part of your career now instead and do not fear condemnation. For veterans who have a hard time of letting go of their past experiences or career, understand its ok, let go of the old ways and embrace the culture of Christ and where you now serve full time. You are not under an oath or orders, you are under grace. This does not minimize your past or patriotism; it transforms your present. Your story does not end with a discharge it will continue in spiritual service and freedom.

Personal Inspection

What ways has your career or past held you back from being bold and confident in expressing your faith?

Prayer
Jesus, thank You for setting me free from condemnation. Help me live like someone who has truly been forgiven and brough forth into a new life.

Day 2

Mission Insight
Condemnation can paralyze a soul. It feels like a yell of, "You're disqualified. You're too far gone." We who have born a lot of our character from our military service may have a tendency of being too hard on ourselves and think we aren't worthy now. But Paul says there's *no* condemnation in Christ, none, you are worthy!

Personal Inspection
What voice of condemnation do you need to silence today with this truth?

Prayer
Lord, shut down the lies that say I am beyond Your grace. Help me live free with you by my side.

Day 3

Mission Insight
This verse does not promise there is no consequence. But it does promise there is no eternal condemnation. You may still be working through consequences, but the penalty, feeling separation from God, identifying as guilty is gone. Those of us walking through healing for whatever ails us can find peace in that.

Personal Inspection

What's the difference between accepting consequences and carrying condemnation?

Prayer

God, help me learn from my past without letting it define me. Let Your grace be my anchor, not shame.

Day 4

Mission Insight

This promise is for those in Christ Jesus, and the key is relationship with Christ. Even if you have had only one assignment or a hundred you know the power of belonging to a team, a unit, or a service. In Christ, you belong to something greater and that belonging secures your freedom.

Personal Inspection

How does your relationship with Christ secure your identity even when you fall short?

Prayer

Jesus, remind me that I am Yours, not because I earned it, but because You claimed me in love.

Day 5

Mission Insight

You cannot live free if you still think you are condemned. It changes how you pray, serve, and love. You've led with strength in uniform now with that same strength lead with humility in grace receiving forgiveness for anything holding you back so you can be all in for God and not held back by your past.

Personal Inspection

What would your life look like if you fully believed you were no longer condemned?

Prayer

Lord, rewire how I see myself. Let freedom replace fear. Let grace replace guilt.

Day 6

Mission Insight

This freedom is not earned it is given, paid forward by Jesus. That is why the cross matters, Jesus took the condemnation so you would not have to. You time in service has trained you to earn everything, as a result you need to hear this truth, salvation is not achieved by performance, but received by faith, there is nothing stopping you but yourself, God is waiting.

Personal Inspection

Where are you still trying to "earn" what Jesus already gave you?

Prayer

God, I lay down my striving trying to earn or be worthy. I receive with thanksgiving what You have already paid for.

Day 7 After-Action Reflection

This week reminds us that we are free to live a spiritual life in Him. If you are in Christ, there is no condemnation, not just less, but absolutely none. That means you can stop replaying the past, punishing yourself, or hiding from grace; you are worthy. God gave his only Son to die for us, that is how much you are worth to God, and how valuable you are. Jesus didn't just die for your sin He rose to give you freedom. Let that truth change how you walk, pray, lead, and love.

Auxiliary Scriptures

- *John 3:17* "God did not send His Son into the world to condemn the world..."
- *Psalm 103:12* "As far as the east is from the west..."

Prayer

Jesus, I believe that because of You, I am not condemned by sin. Help me walk in freedom today unashamed, unafraid, and unburdened due to Your grace.

Field Note

Captain Eddie Rickenbacker, WWI flying ace, Medal of Honor recipient, and man of great faith, survived 24 days adrift at sea after a plane crash during WWII. After 8 days he and his men ran out of food and water, and by a miracle a seagull landed on Rickenbacker's head; he caught it, fed the men and used some as bait to catch fish, beginning the cycle that saved their lives. (Leigh 2013) Like Romans 8:1, his story serves as testament that no life is beyond redemption and no matter the circumstances we find ourselves in, we can all be saved through Christ.

WEEK 29 † ENDURING HARDSHIP

Key Verse: *2 Timothy 2:3 (ESV)*

"Share in suffering as a good soldier of Christ Jesus."

Day 1

Mission Insight

Paul writes to Timothy like a seasoned commander encouraging a new recruit. He does not offer soft platitudes, he calls Timothy to share in suffering as a soldier of Christ. Service members understand this, military life includes sacrifice, hardship, and a commitment greater than comfort. The Christian life is not about ease it is about endurance, mission, and loyalty to the Commander. Paul reminds us that suffering for Christ is not a sign of failure it is a sign of faithfulness and honor.

Personal Inspection

What would you say about you, are you willing to suffer sacrifices for Christ as He did for you?

Prayer

Lord, strengthen me for the fight ahead. Help me suffer well, serve faithfully, and endure like a soldier under Your command for Your greater purpose.

Day 2

Mission Insight

Hardship is part of the mission not a detour from it. Ask any veteran, they didn't expect comfort during deployments; we did what the mission dictated. Likewise, Paul calls us to endure suffering with Christ, knowing it has purpose and reward in the mission Christ has for us.

Personal Inspection

What hard thing in your life might be part of your calling, not a distraction from it?

Prayer

Jesus, give me strength to endure the assignment You've given me even if it is hard I will serve you honorably and stand resolute.

Day 3

Mission Insight

No soldier fights alone. One of the greatest strengths in the military is camaraderie, someone having your six. The same is true spiritually. You were not meant to suffer in silence or isolation like we discussed earlier that many of us are tempted to do. Rather, Paul tells us do not suffer alone, stand together with those who share your faith.

Personal Inspection

Who do you trust to walk with you in your hardest moments and who needs you to do the same?

Prayer

God, thank You for fellow soldiers of the faith. Help me lean on them and be someone they can lean on too.

Day 4

Mission Insight
Endurance does not always look heroic. Sometimes it is getting out of bed, showing up for your family, praying when you don't feel like it, refusing to quit when quitting feels easier. That is not only soldiering on that's also faith, in action.

Personal Inspection
What small act of endurance today is part of your larger fight of faith?

Prayer
Lord, strengthen me for today's task. Help me see endurance as worship, not just survival.

Day 5

Mission Insight
We as a people know that hardship leaves a mark, yet Paul reminds us it can also build character. Suffering for the sake of Christ refines us, deepens us, and draws us closer to the One who suffered first. We're not just called to suffer we are called to suffer for a purpose.

Personal Inspection
How has suffering shaped your spiritual maturity, how has those trials strengthened you?

Prayer
Jesus, do not let my pain go to waste. Use it to shape me into someone who reflects Your strength.

Day 6

Mission Insight

A warrior obeys out of loyalty, and conviction, not convenience. Faith is not about doing what feels good it's about staying true when it costs, taking the hard right, not the easy way out. Paul calls us not to a casual belief but to committed endurance (just as Paul did), one that honors Christ and ourselves.

Personal Inspection

Where is God calling you to stay faithful, even when it is inconvenient?

Prayer

Lord, build loyalty in me. Help me follow You even when I am tired, tested, or tempted to walk an easier path, let me never forget the reward that awaits at the end of my run.

Day 7 After-Action Reflection

This week has been a call to toughness but not the world's version. Spiritual toughness looks like surrender, loyalty, and endurance. You are a true believer, a warrior under orders from a King who walked the hard road first. Suffering is not failure, it's transformative. Stand strong, stay faithful, and remember you are never alone in the fight.

Auxiliary Scriptures

- *Philippians 1:29* "It has been granted to you… to suffer for His sake."
- *Romans 5:3–4* "Suffering produces endurance…"

Prayer

Jesus, thank You for leading me with compassion and courage. Help me endure hardship with grace and to honor You as a faithful soldier of the cross.

Field Note

Sergeant Alvin C. York, one of the most decorated American soldiers of WWI, began as a conscientious objector and a man dedicated to scripture. But after prayer and wrestling with his faith, he chose to serve, believing it was God's will and purpose for him at the time. He did so with unmatched bravery, capturing 132 enemy soldiers in a single battle. York didn't glorify violence; he glorified obedience to his faith even in wartime. (Flick 2022) His courage under fire and conviction under pressure reflect 2 Timothy 2:3: endure hardship, not to prove yourself, but to honor and glorify the One you serve.

WEEK 30 † GOD IS OUR REFUGE

Key Verse: *Psalm 46:1 (ESV)*

"God is our refuge and strength, a very present help in trouble."

Day 1

Mission Insight

A powerful declaration God is not distant, detached, or delayed. He is right here, right now and He is both refuge and strength. A concept we have visited in other weeks put important to revisit again. We know the chaos of war or living through mobilizations, the tough decisions in leadership positions, or the internal battles that rage long after the mission ends. In those moments, it is tempting to look for shelter in distractions, substances, or isolation (there is isolation again). But Psalm 46 points us back to the only refuge that never fails. God is not just nearby He is active, available, and strong enough to carry that pack or that payload that you cannot alone.

Personal Inspection

What is your refuge you go to in trouble, how have you coped, is God first in your answer?

Prayer
Lord, thank You for being my refuge in times of trouble. Teach me to run to You, not from You; Teach me to come to you first in times of trouble and not last.

Day 2

Mission Insight
A refuge is more than a place to hide it's a place to be held. Take it from us who have spent time in bunkers or shelters during attack or indirect fire, we know how precious protection feels in that moment. God offers that kind of presence, not to remove us from the storm, but to shield us in it.

Personal Inspection
What storm are you walking through and how can you run to God as your shelter?

Prayer
God, I need more than just answers I need Your covering and hardened protection in the storm. Be my safety, power, and strength today.

Day 3

Mission Insight
Strength and refuge go together. God is both your protection and your source of energy to keep going. We've been trained to find a way and push through, but there's strength in knowing when to also rest in God, recharge in His presence, and then move forward.

Personal Inspection

Where are you running on empty and how can God's strength fill the gap?

Prayer

Lord, I find parts of me are tired. Strengthen me from within and restore what has been depleted so that I may continue the good fight.

Day 4

Mission Insight

"Very present" means more than hanging out smoking and joking. It means right there and attentive. Some veterans feel forgotten by the world, by the system, even by the church. But God hasn't forgotten you. He sees, hears, and is right there with you, in all times, not just your time of need, but he's there too.

Personal Inspection

Where have you felt unseen and how might God be meeting you in that very place. When you look where is He, when you listen what is He telling you?

Prayer

Jesus, meet me in the places I have felt abandoned. Remind me that You never turn away but are there even more with me.

Day 5

Mission Insight

When trouble comes, your first instinct matters. Do you run to God or something else? We can be guilty of sometimes carrying go-to responses from our years of constant training. But spiritually, we are invited to retrain that instinct and habitual response, and turn to God first, not last.

Personal Inspection
What do you normally turn to when things get hard and how can you turn to God instead. If you turn to God first how might that make a difference in the outcome?

Prayer
Lord, make Yourself my first call in crisis not my backup plan, for You created the universe and this world, who would know better than You, please open my ears and heart to hear You.

Day 6

Mission Insight
God is our refuge, not might be, but is! Present tense. Whether you are in a hospital bed, at a graveside, in a courtroom, or at home in silence God is still refuge. Trouble does not cancel His presence, rather it reveals it.

Personal Inspection
How have you seen God's presence show up in unexpected places?

Prayer
Father, thank You that my circumstances do not define Your faithfulness, help me see You, even in the chaos.

Day 7 After-Action Reflection

This week reminded us that trouble is real but so is God. You don't have to downplay your pain or pretend everything is okay. But you also don't have to walk through it alone. God is your refuge, He is your strength, He is your very present help. Veterans, those still in, and civilians alike need that reminder, not just in crisis, but every day.

Auxiliary Scriptures

- *Nahum 1:7* "The Lord is good, a stronghold in the day of trouble..."
- *Isaiah 41:10* "Fear not, for I am with you..."

Prayer

God, thank You for being near, when I feel vulnerable, You are my refuge; when I feel weak, You are my strength. I trust You today completely and without reservation.

Field Note

Father Karl-Albert Lindblad, CHC, US Navy, during the 9/11 attacks was the first Navy Chaplain on scene at Ground Zero to minister amid chaos and destruction. In the ash and debris, he walked with firefighters, first responders, and families, offering prayer, counsel, and presence. He was present to offer comfort, help guide rescuers, and assist in getting a Navy hospital ship to New York Harbor. ("Catholic Military Chaplain Who Witnessed 9/11 Sees Goodness in National Unity 10 Years Later - Archdiocese for the Military, USA" 2011) Like Psalm 46:1, his presence pointed to a greater presence; the God who stands steady in times of trouble, even when the world seems to collapse around us.

WEEK 31 † WORK FOR THE LORD

Key Verse: *Colossians 3:23 (ESV)*

"Whatever you do, work heartily, as for the Lord and not for men."

Day 1

Mission Insight

This verse reframes everyday labor as sacred. Written to believers, many of whom were servants or in difficult social positions; Paul calls them to see their work not as obligation, but as worship. This message brings purpose to even the most mundane tasks. Whether you're in a war room, boardroom, warehouse, or in transition, your work matters; not because others are watching, but because God is. He's your real boss. And He values diligence, faithfulness, and heart. When you work for the Lord, there's no wasted effort.

Personal Inspection

What drives you every day, is it primarily for the attention of other people, or in service of Christ?

Prayer

Lord, help me see my work as service to You. Whether it is noticed or not, let me do it with heart and honor because I know that You see all.

Day 2

Mission Insight

Veterans understand chain of command. You follow orders even when you disagree. Paul lifts our eyes above any earthly supervisor and reminds us that God is our ultimate authority. That gives dignity to any role and excellence to every effort, in Him is our purpose.

Personal Inspection

How would your attitude shift if you saw your current task as directly assigned by God?

Prayer

Jesus, help me work today with the mindset that You are my Commander, and I serve You first.

Day 3

Mission Insight

Heartily means "from the soul." This is not about just work it's about genuineness. Military members sometime struggle with "take a knee" positions or Veterans sometimes struggle in civilian jobs that feel less mission driven or serve with those who are less driven in general. But God's Word reminds us, mission is not about the task it's about why and how you do it. If it is for the Lord, it is never meaningless and always purposeful; ensure you make God part of whatever you are doing!

Personal Inspection

What would it look like to approach your job or do your work "from the soul" this week?

Prayer
God, put purpose in my heart, not just productivity in my hands. Help me work with joy and be reminded throughout that I ultimately work for You.

Day 4

Mission Insight
"Not for men." That is the challenge. Most of us crave recognition or fear rejection trying to fit into the culture of today. We all learned and know the power of counseling, performance reviews, and evaluations. But God invites us to step off the treadmill of people-pleasing and find freedom in serving Him first, and if you do, the reward will be greater than anything a person can say about you.
Self-Reflection
What pressure are you feeling to impress people, where are you exerting energy towards societal conformity and how can you redirect that focus and energy toward God?

Prayer
Lord, I want to serve You, not perform for others, center my motives and guard my heart.

Day 5

Mission Insight
God values all kinds of work. Leading a team, changing a diaper, caring for an aging parent, mentoring youth, feeding the hungry, sharing knowledge, helping someone move, etc. It is all sacred when done for Him. Veterans specifically sometimes feel aimless after service, but this verse redeems every task. If it's done in love, and ultimately for the One, it counts.

Personal Inspection
What ordinary or common place tasks do you need to see today as sacred?

Prayer
Jesus, give me vision to see the holy in the humble. Let me work with meaning, not just motion.

Day 6

Mission Insight
This kind of heart work does not always feel rewarding. Sometimes you serve faithfully, and no one sees. But God sees, He rewards the private acts of service in this life and the next. Anyone who has done the hard unnoticed jobs can take comfort, your faithfulness never goes unseen or unappreciated in heaven, and that should be the root motivation for all that we do!

Personal Inspection
Where have you been faithful without recognition and how does God's approval satisfy more than man's?

Prayer
God, I trust that You see me in all that I do, let that be enough when no one else does.

Day 7 After-Action Reflection

This week reminded us that work when done for God becomes worship. Whether you are in a new role, between assignments, or serving in unseen ways, your faithfulness matters. We have been trained to know that every position contributes to the mission, and God tells us in the Kingdom, it's no different. When you work with heart, you reflect the heart of the One who called you.

Auxiliary Scriptures

- *1 Corinthians 10:31* "Whatever you do… do all to the glory of God."
- *Galatians 6:9* "Let us not grow weary of doing good…"

Prayer

Lord, whatever I do today let it honor You, make my work meaningful because of who I do it for.

Field Note

St. Joan of Arc (1412–1431), a teenage French peasant girl lived by dedicating her life and work fully to God. At the time France was internally fractured and at war with England and Joan believed she was called by God to lead her nation. Despite her lack of training, status, or worldly power, she courageously convinced military leaders to give her command. Her leadership helped lift the siege of Orléans in 1429, a pivotal moment in the war. Joan consistently believed her mission was not for personal glory but for God and country. Even at her trial, when offered safety in exchange for renouncing her convictions, she stood firm and was burned at the stake at just 19 years old. ("St. Joan of Arc - FaithND" 2024) Joan's life reflected Colossians 3:23: she worked with all her heart for God, not for men, and her legacy of courage and devotion endures across centuries.

WEEK 32 † WISDOM FOR LIFE'S DECISIONS

Key Verse: *James 1:5 (ESV)*

"If any of you lacks wisdom, let him ask God, who gives generously to all without reproach, and it will be given him."

Day 1

Mission Insight

This verse offers clear and simple guidance from a trustworthy Creator, if you lack wisdom ask and He will give it generously. Those of us navigating big transitions, new careers, strained relationships, trauma of some sort, or spiritual questions, this verse says one thing; you do not have to figure it all out alone. God does not shame you for not knowing He invites your request. The wisdom He gives is insight rooted in His character, shaped by His Spirit, and designed for real-life application. The question isn't whether you qualify for wisdom It is whether you will ask for it and have ears to hear when God speaks.

Personal Inspection

Where might you be lacking in humility to admit that "I don't know" and let go of control and ask God for the answer?

Prayer

Lord, I do not always know what to do. Teach me to come to You first when I need wisdom and trust that You will provide it.

Day 2

Mission Insight

Wisdom is not the same as knowledge. You can have a head full of facts and still make foolish choices, I and many still do this in our own lives. Godly wisdom is about discernment knowing when to act, when to wait, and how to choose the path of righteousness. Veterans, in any sense of the word who've made important and even life-or-death decisions know the value of calm clarity. God offers that not just in crisis, but every day.

Personal Inspection

What decision are you facing right now where you need God's wisdom not just human advice?

Prayer

God, speak clearly where I am uncertain and let me hear Your will for me. Make my next step wise, not just practical from my own limited worldly understanding.

Day 3

Mission Insight

The verse says God gives "generously to all without reproach." That means He doesn't roll His eyes when you ask, He does not say, "You should know this by now." People (especially those in our line of work) used to being the ones with answers or afraid to admit they do not know can struggle to ask for help, but this kind of asking is strength and empowerment, not weakness.

Personal Inspection

He is the Alpha and the Omega and The Creator of the all things, so what is keeping you from asking God for wisdom more regularly?

Prayer

Lord, thank You that You never shame me for needing help. Make me humble enough to ask and patient enough to wait for Your answer.

Day 4

Mission Insight

God's wisdom often looks different than the world's, it is slow to anger, full of mercy, peaceable, and pure (James 3:17). When trained to act decisively you may need to re-learn a different rhythm such as pausing, praying, then moving in peace. Tactical patience is not just for the battlefield or a training exercise it is also for moving forward in faith; it is not hesitation it is a sign of wisdom.

Personal Inspection

Where have you been following the world's way and the world's pace of decision-making instead of God's?

Prayer

Jesus, reset my instincts. Let Your wisdom shape how I lead, speak, and respond.

Day 5

Mission Insight
God's wisdom comes through multiple channels be it prayer, Scripture, wise counsel, and the Holy Spirit's prompting (are you listening?). If you've ever relied on solid intel or trusted advisors as I am sure you have, then you should treat spiritual wisdom the same way, seek sources that are reliable and align with God's truth.

Personal Inspection
Where are you seeking wisdom right now and are those sources pointing you toward God?

Prayer
God, guide me through the voices I hear. Let the ones that speak Your truth rise above the rest.

Day 6

Mission Insight
Sometimes we don't ask for wisdom because we are afraid of what God might say. But wisdom from God is truth and He wants to and will walk with you through uncertainty. Asking Him for wisdom isn't about getting control it's about gaining trust to take the correct path.

Personal Inspection
What area of your life do you need to stop trying to control and start trusting God for wisdom?

Prayer
Lord, I surrender my need to have all the answers. Give me wisdom and peace in the unknown.

Day 7 After-Action Reflection

This week reminded us that God is not silent and He's not stingy. When you need wisdom, you can ask; when you ask, He gives. If you are navigating complex transitions or deep personal questions you can rest in knowing you are not expected to figure it all out alone. The One who designed your life is eager to guide your steps. So ask boldly, listen humbly, and walk wisely.

Auxiliary Scriptures

- *Proverbs 3:5–6* "In all your ways acknowledge Him, and He will make straight your paths."
- *Isaiah 30:21* "Your ears shall hear a word behind you, saying, 'This is the way, walk in it.'"

Prayer

Father, I need Your wisdom more than ever. Lead me when I am unsure. Remind me that You are generous with those who ask, help me hear and follow.

Field Note

Baron von Steuben, an experienced Prussian military officer met with General Washington at Valley Forge in 1778. Upon his inspection of the men and conditions, he found everything lacking minus their spirit. Seeking help and experienced wisdom to organize a fighting force, General Washington employed Von Steuben to train his Army. The seeking of help beyond General Washington's own abilities played a vital role in the Continental Army's victory over the British. (National park service 2016) This example embodies the message found in James 1:5: seek wisdom from God; do not only rely solely on your own understanding. It can change everything!

WEEK 33 † RESTORATION AFTER SUFFERING

Key Verse: *1 Peter 5:10 (ESV)*

"And after you have suffered a little while, the God of all grace, who has called you to his eternal glory in Christ, will himself restore, confirm, strengthen, and establish you."

Day 1

Mission Insight

A follow on to Week 16, Peter wrote this to believers under persecution, people who knew pain and uncertainty. His words resonate for both service members and civilians who have also walked through suffering, both seen and unseen. This verse does not deny hardship it advocates resiliency through it. "After you have suffered" acknowledges the reality of pain, but the promise is stronger and more eternal than the pain; God will "restore, confirm, strengthen, and establish you". The suffering will not last but God's grace will, He is the One who heals, steadies, and rebuilds what the world has torn down.

Personal Inspection

Have you asked "Why me", "Why now", have you then said after "where to now God, lead the way"?

Prayer
God, I do not always understand the suffering I am walking through, but I trust that You are not finished! Restore and strengthen me today so that I may continue marching on for Your Glory.

Day 2

Mission Insight
The phrase "a little while" can feel insulting when you've been suffering for a while. But Peter isn't minimizing your pain He is magnifying eternity. All who have endured long stretches of adversity can find hope here, your current struggle is not the end of your story, not even close, keep the faith.

Personal Inspection
What hardship feels endless right now and how might this verse give you eternal perspective?

Prayer
Lord, help me lift my eyes beyond today's pain. Anchor me in the hope of what You are still doing and will do.

Day 3

Mission Insight
God does not outsource your healing, He Himself will restore you. If you are used to fixing things alone heed this reminder; that you my good friend, are not your own redeemer. Let God do what only He can do, His restoration is personal, intentional, customized, and full of grace and he can do more than you can ever do alone.

Personal Inspection

Where in your life are you trying to restore yourself your way, rather than trusting God's way. What can you do to learn more about the Word and less about the world?

Prayer

Father, I give You access to all of me even the broken places, restore me Your way not mine.

Day 4

Mission Insight

Did you notice each verb is a promise: restore what was lost, confirm what is true, strengthen what is weak, and establish what will last. You all who feel stripped down after service or a tough assignment can take comfort God is not just rehabilitating you, He is rebuilding you for something new.

Personal Inspection

Which part of this verse do you most need today, restoration, confirmation, strength, or stability?

Prayer

Jesus, meet me in the place I feel weakest, I trust You to fix, refurbish, rebuild what I cannot adequately on my own without You.

Day 5

Mission Insight

This promise comes from "the God of all grace." Not some grace, but absolutely ALL grace. That means no wound is too deep, no failure too far gone. Whatever burdens it is you carry in your baggage;

know His grace and light reach deeper than your darkest places, there is no abyss for God, no chasm he cannot grasp into and recover you from.

Personal Inspection

You are worthy, so what area of your life needs the touch of "all grace" today?

Prayer

God, pour out Your grace, a love I do not have to earn but accept, on every part of me especially the places I still try to hide.

Day 6

Mission Insight

This promise is not just about stamina, it's about transformation. Military personnel past and present who have survived service or an enlistment may ask, "Now what?" The answer is here, simple, God's not finished. Transitioning or re-upping, He's establishing something stronger in you than what you have established in yourself thus far.

Personal Inspection

How might God be using your past suffering to build something stronger in your character?

Prayer

Lord, use my scars not just to remind me of where I've been, but to show me where You are taking me; keep my eyes focused forward on the path You've set before me.

Day 7 After-Action Reflection

This week reminded us that suffering is real but so is God's restoration. You have not been abandoned. You have been *called.* You have not been ruined you are ready to be restored. We need to acknowledge going forward; no pain is wasted, and no journey is too off course for God to rebuild us or redirect us. He will strengthen what is weak, steady what is shaken, and confirm what's eternal. This is grace and it is personal to you.

Auxiliary Scriptures

- *Romans 5:3–5* "Suffering produces endurance… and hope does not put us to shame."
- *Isaiah 61:3* "To give them beauty for ashes…"

Prayer

God of all grace, thank You that I am not forgotten. Restore what has been lost or broken, confirm what is true, and build my life on the foundation of Your goodness.

Field Note

Major Richard "Dick" Winters, commander of Easy Company, 506th PIR, 101st Airborne, during WWII (may sound familiar and if like me, you're a fan of "Band of Brothers"), endured brutal combat in Normandy, Operation Market Garden, and the Battle of the Bulge. After the war, Winters lived a quiet life, never seeking glory but seeking normalcy and peace. Despite a statue erected in his honor at Normandy, he remained humble and denied being a hero, but said he served with heroes. His post-war life exemplified restoration, strength from suffering and stability after chaos. ("MAJ Richard D. Winters," n.d.) As 1 Peter 5:10 promises, God had not just seen Winters through battle, He established him in grace and legacy far beyond war.

WEEK 34 † HOPE AFTER HARDSHIP

Key Verse: *Job 11:16-19 (ESV)*

> **"You will forget your misery; you will remember it as waters that have passed away. And your life will be brighter than the noonday; its darkness will be like the morning. And you will feel secure, because there is hope…"**

Day 1

Mission Insight

This verse comes from one of Job's friends, offering a glimpse of hope amidst deep suffering. It reflects and reinforces what we have read before, suffering will not last forever. For young and old alike who have lived through darkness, service related or otherwise, these words speak healing. There is life beyond pain, misery will one day feel like "waters that have passed." Hope doesn't erase what happened, but it allows Christ to work so your future can shine brighter than your past.

Personal Inspection

What makes todays troubles different from yours 10 years ago? God got you through those as He will get you through any you face today; and like those troubles of the past, they too will be distant memories.

Prayer
Lord, thank You that my darkest days do not define my future. Let Your hope reshape how I see what is ahead and allow You to work in me.

Day 2

Mission Insight
"You will forget your misery…" does not mean denial it means healed distance. Like fading scars, the pain loses its sharpness over time. As my father would tell me time heals all, I now know how this works, because it allows God time to work in our lives. You may wonder if you will ever move past whatever pains you? This verse offers a sacred "yes", by God's grace.

Personal Inspection
What hardship feels permanent to you and how might God be slowly turning it into a passing memory?

Prayer
God, I do not want to forget my story I want to heal from it. Turn my past into a testimony, that inspires my onward movement to the mission you have before me.

Day 3

Mission Insight
"Your life will be brighter than the noonday." That is not just pie in the sky talk, it is a promise. We who have lived long in emotional or spiritual darkness need this reminder, God can and will bring light again, Joy will return. Dawn will always break, even after a long night; remember it is darkest before the dawn.

Personal Inspection

Where is light needed to break through in your life today how can you help God's light to shine?

Prayer

Jesus, shine brightly on the places in me that have stayed dark for too long change my perspective. I want to hope again, and through Your grace and guidance I know I will.

Day 4

Mission Insight

"You will feel secure, because there is hope." So often we reverse this thinking we need security before we can hope. But God says, hope produces security, be optimistic and believe (trust) in God's plan. Warriors on land, air, sea, or space used to being alert for threats must learn to rest in the hope that Christ brings, and less hypervigilant on what could go wrong.

Personal Inspection

What would it take for you to feel secure in hope even when you don't have total control?

Prayer

Lord, I give You my anxiety. Anchor me in a hope that steadies me and allows me to be vulnerable to You.

Day 5

Mission Insight

Hope is hard when you have experienced a loss of something in life. This verse reminds us that the future is not built on pains absence, it's built on the presence of God. While navigating hardship, loneliness, regret, or emptiness, you are not disqualified from joy. Your future is still wide open, hope and faithfulness in the Lord let this time pass like the waters, and great things yet await.

Personal Inspection

What new future might God be inviting you to believe is still possible, what is He telling you?

Prayer

Father, help me believe that something good is still ahead of me even if I cannot see it yet, let me never forget that I have a purpose and you have a plan.

Day 6

Mission Insight

"You will lie down, and none will make you afraid." For anyone used to sleeping where a threat persists 24/7 or carrying internal tension and anxiety, this promise hits home. God offers peace not just for eternity, but for tonight. A Safe rest, unworried sleep, deep security in His hope.

Personal Inspection

What would true rest look like for you and what might be keeping you from receiving it?

Prayer

God, give me rest. Let me lie down tonight without fear, covered by Your peace. Let me not forget my faith and belief in You ensuring that you will forever be my shepherd and protector.

Day 7 After-Action Reflection

This week reminded us that hope is not just wishful thinking it's God's pathway to healing. Misery may still echo, but it will one day fade, darkness will turn to dawn, and fear will yield to peace. If you are carrying the weight of old battles external or internal you have been promised, healing is possible, rest is available, and hope remains alive through the Holy Spirit.

Auxiliary Scriptures

- *Psalm 30:5* "Weeping may tarry for the night, but joy comes with the morning."
- *Romans 15:13* "May the God of hope fill you with all joy and peace in believing…"

Prayer

Jesus, thank You that hope is stronger than memory. Rewrite my story with Your grace, and lead me toward peace, joy, and rest that lasts.

Field Note

Captain Ernest Gordon, a Scottish officer captured during WWII, endured brutal conditions in a Japanese POW camp while building the Burma Railway. Initially near death, Gordon witnessed a quiet spiritual revival among prisoners, men sacrificing their lives for one another, and worshiping in faith together. As he healed physically, he was also transformed spiritually, later becoming a pastor and author. ("Cana Academy," n.d.) His story echoes Job 11:16–19: from suffering came hope, from despair came renewal, and from one man's misery came a legacy of service to God.

WEEK 35 † GOD HOLDS YOUR HAND

Key Verse: *Isaiah 41:9-13 (ESV)*

"I have chosen you and not cast you off; fear not, for I am with you; be not dismayed, for I am your God; I will strengthen you, I will help you, I will uphold you with my righteous right hand…."

Day 1

Mission Insight

Used as an auxiliary reference previously, these words spoken through the prophet Isaiah, are God's personal assurance to those who feel abandoned or overwhelmed. Many people who have experienced separation, trauma, or a sense of being discarded, even feeling out of place can resonate deeply with this truth: ***God has not cast you off.*** He chooses, strengthens, helps, and upholds. He does not do it from a distance; He holds your hand. That is intimate, close, an unwavering presence. When fear rises, when strength fails, when the mission feels uncertain, you are not alone. The Commander of Heaven walks beside you, sustaining your every step.

Personal Inspection

When God tries to hold your hand, do you let him take it, or are you still missing out on being held up?

Prayer
Father, thank You that I have not been cast off. When I am afraid, hold my hand in assurance and strengthen me to keep moving forward.

Day 2

Mission Insight
"I have chosen you." That is Christ's personally identifying you. Not because of rank, performance, or flawless behavior but because of His love. Service members often struggle with a shifting sense of worth after service or in the civilian side of their lives, but God's choice of you is not temporary, it's eternal, there is no end to his love for you and the Holy Spirit's presence in your life.

Personal Inspection
Where are you questioning your worth and how does God's choice sure up your identity?

Prayer
Lord, remind me that You chose me not for what I have done, but because of who You are.

Day 3

Mission Insight
"Fear not, for I am with you." These words are not a pep talk they are a call out of His reassuring presence. Those who have felt alone, isolated or unseen need this assurance. God's nearness is not a metaphor it's not a comforting concept, It is a reality. Even in the darkest rooms, the most silent battles, or any other place you can think of, He is there.

Personal Inspection

What situation right now makes you feel alone and how have you been missing God's presence?

Prayer

God, I do not need You to remove every fear I just need You close as I face it. Thank You for being with me and making all things possible and for including me in "all things".

Day 4

Mission Insight

"I will strengthen you, I will help you, I will uphold you." That is triple coverage like bubble wrap, Styrofoam, and packing peanuts all in one. God does not just encourage, you are actually sustained, held up by His strength. Again, addressing those who have served and our propensity for self-reliance we must learn this holy dependence... your strongest place is in His grip, hand in hand.

Personal Inspection

Where have you been standing on your own, how can you let God hold you up and be stronger?

Prayer

Lord, hold me steady when I'm weak or listing the wrong way. I do not want to depend on my understanding alone, I want to trust Your strength and live true to Your way not mine.

Day 5

Mission Insight

"Be not dismayed." Dismay is more than being disheartened its being disoriented as well, the feeling of being spiritually or emotionally unmoored. Any of us who have ever had a plan or a perceived self-perception then know that feeling when plans collapse (after-all we know no plan survives first contact) or identity shifts. But God steadies the heart. He does not just get us through He gets us back on the right track and helps us define our true selves.

Personal Inspection

What's disoriented you lately from your faith and how can you let God be your grounding point?

Prayer

Jesus, when I feel lost, shaken, or even my best laid plans fall apart, be my compass. Set my feet back on solid ground.

Day 6

Mission Insight

"For I… hold your right hand." God does not push from behind or pull from ahead, He walks right beside you. Hand-in-hand, side by side, like how a parent guides a child, or a brother steadies a wounded friend. That is God's posture toward you. He can work ahead of you and be at your side the whole time, remember nearness, he is always near even when working afar.

Personal Inspection

Where in your life do you need to feel the steady grip of God's hand?

Prayer
Father, I reach for You today. Take my hand, walk with me in strength, peace, and help carry me when I am wounded or stumble so that I may regain my feet and continue on the right path.

Day 7 After-Action Reflection

This week reminded us that God's faithfulness is both fierce and tender. Any souls who have felt forgotten, unstable, or afraid now hear God tell them they are chosen to be with Him. God is present in fear, strong in weakness, and close enough to hold your hand. Whatever you face never forget that His grip doesn't slip, His strength does not fade, His presence is everlasting.

Auxiliary Scriptures

- *Psalm 73:23–24* "I am continually with you; you hold my right hand."
- *2 Corinthians 12:9* "My grace is sufficient for you, for my power is made perfect in weakness."

Prayer
God, thank You for not letting go when I falter, strengthen me when I fear, steady me helping me walk in peace; held by Your hand and I will journey this life with You and for You.

Field Note

Corrie ten Boom, a Dutch Christian watchmaker's daughter during World War II, exemplified courage and faith. When the Nazis occupied the Netherlands, Corrie and her family sheltered Jews in their home, saving hundreds of lives. Eventually, she and her family were arrested and sent to concentration camps, where her father would later die. Despite brutal conditions, she encouraged others to trust that God had not abandoned them. Corrie survived the camp and after the war, she traveled the world sharing her testimony, including the power of forgiveness. (Ten Boom et al. 2015) She exemplified Isaiah 41:9–13 in her book "The Hiding Place," where she wrote, "There is no pit so deep, that God's love is not deeper still."

WEEK 36 † THE ULTIMATE SACRIFICE

Key Verse: *John 3:16 (ESV)*

"For God so loved the world, that he gave his only Son, that whoever believes in him should not perish but have eternal life."

Day 1

Mission Insight

This statement by Jesus to Nicodemus is the cornerstone of the Christian faith and perhaps the most quoted verse in all of Scripture. But it is more than a slogan or stadium sign reference. It is a declaration of sacrificial love, offered not to the deserving, but to the broken. You understand sacrifice having given deeply in so many ways. John 3:16 reveals God Himself entered the fight, sacrificing His Son for the rescue of humanity. In Christ, we receive not just forgiveness, but eternal life. That is how much we matter to God.

Personal Inspection

What does it mean to you that God sacrificed Jesus to be the last sacrifice ever needed for your salvation?

Prayer

Father, thank You for loving me with a love so deeply that you gave us your Son so that He may sacrifice Himself for us and our salvation. Help me receive that love and live from it daily.

Day 2

Mission Insight

"God so loved…" Love, not judgment. Veterans and service members who struggle with post service or post deployment life can be reassured that God still loves them, unconditionally and without fail. God did not send Jesus to punish us He sent Him to save us. Love is what moved Him, and His love is what sustains us. The take away, short and sweet is know that you are loved, despite all else God will always love you.

Personal Inspection

Where do you need to admit to, recognize, believe, and receive God's love for you today?

Prayer

Lord, teach me to accept Your love, not just acknowledge it in Scripture. Let it sink deep and shape everything I am and become part of how I see myself and my own worth.

Day 3

Mission Insight

"That whoever believes…" There are no restrictions, no Base or Post Exchange privileges needed, no background checks, no prerequisites. God's offer is for whoever and that means ALL. Some may feel disqualified by their past or they feel disconnected, but the invitation is still open and remains valid. Being able to believe isn't about perfection, it is about genuine faith in Christ and why he came for you.

Personal Inspection
What fear or failure has made you feel disqualified and how does this verse challenge that?

Prayer
Jesus, I bring my whole story good and bad, I need to admit to myself you already know it all and there is nothing to hide from you. With all that I still believe You still want me.

Day 4

Mission Insight
"He gave His only Son." That is not symbolic it's the ultimate gift from God. We have seen our comrades in arms give their lives for their country, exemplifying that the deepest love is proven in what we are willing to give. God did not just speak love He demonstrated it by giving of Himself. The cross, Christ sacrificing himself, is the receipt of that love.

Personal Inspection
What does it mean to you that God gave His best, His one and only Son, for you?

Prayer
Father, help me grasp the depth of what You gave. Let the cross never feel common to me.

Day 5

Mission Insight
"Should not perish but have eternal life." Eternal life doesn't start at heaven it starts now. It means peace, purpose, and relationship with God today for that tomorrow. Those longing for meaning beyond their service can find a new mission here, living out what Christ died to give us.

Personal Inspection
How might you live differently if you saw eternal life as something you experience now, not just later?

Prayer
God, help me walk in the eternal life You have given me not just waiting for heaven, but living with purpose now.

Day 6

Mission Insight
This verse is an anchor in times of doubt, despair, and disorientation. When everything else feels unstable, your faith, mental health, identity, this promise stands firm. God loves you, He gave everything for you. And through your ardent heartfelt belief in Christ, you have eternal life.

Personal Inspection
When life feels uncertain, how can you return to the foundation of God's love?

Prayer
Lord, be my anchor when I drift. Remind me that no matter what changes, Your love does not.

Day 7 After-Action Reflection

John 3:16 is not just a memory verse, it's your cornerstone. I know you know the weight of sacrifice. This week, we've remembered the One who bore the ultimate cost not for a country, but for the world. Not for the deserving, but for the lost; Jesus' life, death, and resurrection open the door to eternal life for all. And it starts with belief. This verse is an invitation from Christ every day to receive, be saved, and live in His love.

Auxiliary Scriptures

- *Romans 5:8* "God shows His love for us in that while we were still sinners, Christ died for us."
- *1 John 4:9–10* "In this the love of God was made manifest among us…"

Prayer
Jesus, thank You for loving me to the point of death to fulfill scripture and save us all from sin. Help me never get used to the cross and let Your love lead everything I do.

Field Note

Sergeant First Class Alwyn Cashe, 3rd Infantry Division, was posthumously awarded the Medal of Honor for extraordinary heroism in Iraq in 2005. When his Bradley Fighting Vehicle was struck by an IED and engulfed in flames; already badly burned, he repeatedly entered the fiery wreck to rescue six fellow Soldiers and an interpreter.

Despite being severely burned over 75% of his body, he continued heroically and died weeks later from his injuries. ("Sergeant First Class Alwyn C. Cashe," n.d.) Cashe's actions embodied the spirit of John 3:16: a life willingly laid down so others might live; his legacy lives on well beyond his own life.

WEEK 37 † UNSHAKABLE LOVE

Key Verse: *Romans 8:38-39 (ESV)*

"For I am sure that neither death nor life, nor angels nor rulers, nor things present nor things to come, nor powers, nor height nor depth, nor anything else in all creation, will be able to separate us from the love of God in Christ Jesus our Lord."

Day 1

Mission Insight

Paul's declaration in Romans 8 is a spiritual anchor for anyone who has faced death, oppression, persecution or even just uncertainty about the future. For many of us, experiences in combat zones, stressful situations, and relationships created doubts about whether God's love can truly cover everything they have seen or done. But Paul says nothing can separate us. Not death, not governments, not past regrets or future failures. The love of God is not based on your performance it's grounded in Christ's finished work. This is a love stronger than war, deeper than guilt, and wider than fear.

Personal Inspection

Do you truly know that nothing, absolutely nothing can separate you and God, that His love is forever?

Prayer
Father, thank You that nothing, meaning absolutely nothing, can separate me from Your love. Help me believe and live confidently knowing that our relationship is unbreakable for eternity.

Day 2

Mission Insight
Paul says he is sure, a statement not made out of arrogance, but for your assurance. Uncertainty in this world is common, but this truth offers rock-solid confidence that God's love is not unsteady under foot but a place to stand strong in life's spiritual battle. You do not have to fear losing ground even in the worst or most challenging moments, your relationship is inseparable as long as you believe.

Personal Inspection
Do you believe God's love holds you just as tightly on your worst days as on your best?

Prayer
Lord, help me trade insecurity for assurance and let Your love be the most certain part of my life.

Day 3

Mission Insight
"Nor things present nor things to come..." God's love covers your now and always. Veterans transitioning to civilian life or service men and women about to head into harm's way often feel uncertain about what's ahead, yet God already knows. This verse promises the future cannot separate you from God's presence and affection, love Him and you will know His timeless love in return no matter where you are.

Personal Inspection

What future unknowns are weighing on you and how can this promise calm those fears?

Prayer

God, You already hold tomorrow and know the plan help me rest in the promise that I will never face a day outside Your love no matter what may be ahead.

Day 4

Mission Insight

People in general often carry deep emotional weight, possibly from guilt, anger, anxiety, maybe even sorrow or a combination of a few of them. Paul in this verse implies clearly that at the lowest moments of emotional turmoil still are not too low for God's love. There is no depth He won't reach into as we've covered before, but in this verse stresses that God goes where the believer is to ensure that the connection and relationship to Him will always remain intact as long as you truly believe in Him.

Personal Inspection

What "deep" place in your soul still doubts you're loved and what would it mean to let God speak there?

Prayer

Jesus, enter even the hidden, hurting places. Show me that Your love goes deeper still then I have been able to realize and that you are always ready to preserve our connection.

Day 5

Mission Insight

Paul's list is extensive: life, death, powers, height, depth. It's as if he is daring you and me to think of anything that could break God's grip. However, the answer is always the same, nothing can; he flat out tells us there is nothing in all of creation that can. That's the kind of security all of us long for and it's found in Christ; it has been waiting for us this whole time.

Personal Inspection

What do you fear might separate you from God and how does this verse speak to that fear?

Prayer

Lord, when I doubt or wander, pull me back with this truth as Paul has revealed to us, that nothing can separate me from You.

Day 6

Mission Insight

"...in Christ Jesus our Lord." This love is not general or generic it is found exclusively in relationship with Jesus. Being part of a unit, a team, a squad, then you understand loyalty, brother/sisterhood, and shared close experiences will resonate with this kind of love that is committed, personal, and eternal. Jesus is with you through it all, doing battle by your side daily, experiencing your most personal moments, greatest successes, and even colossal failures; Yet He but loves you any way and drives on with you undeterred.

Personal Inspection

What does it mean to you that God's love is not just universal but specifically available to you in Christ?

Prayer

Father, thank You that Your love is personal, that you know me for who I really am and Your love remains unconditional. Let me walk in it today with confidence and humility.

Day 7 After-Action Reflection

This week reminded us that God's love isn't theoretical its real and it is invincible. War, trauma, fear, transition, regret, failure, or worldly success; none of these can separate you from Him. You friend, are not too far gone, too successful, or two broken to begin this forever love with you Savior. In Christ, you are forever held, fully loved, and never alone. This love outlasts every battle, withstands any attack, overcomes the world, and carries you home.

Auxiliary Scriptures

- *Psalm 139:7–10* "Where can I go from your Spirit? … Even there your hand shall lead me."
- *John 10:28–29*—"No one will snatch them out of my hand."

Prayer

God, let Your love be the loudest voice in my heart. Keep me rooted, held, and unshaken because nothing can take me from Your grip.

Field Note

Admiral James Stockdale, a U.S. Navy aviator, Vietnam POW for over seven years, and Medal of Honor recipient, endured brutal captivity with remarkable resilience. While imprisoned, he maintained a leadership role among fellow captives, despite facing solitary confinement, torture, and extreme uncertainty. Stockdale later credited his survival to what was called the "Stockdale Paradox" which is confronting the brutal reality while never losing faith and resilience. ("The Stockdale Paradox – Vibrant Faith" 2022) His unshakable mindset reflected Romans 8:38–39; not hardship nor life's difficult realities can separate us from hope, and one day victory.

WEEK 38 † FREEDOM FROM ANXIETY

Key Verse: *Matthew 6:25-27 (ESV)*

"Therefore I tell you, do not be anxious about your life... Look at the birds of the air: they neither sow nor reap... and yet your heavenly Father feeds them. Are you not of more value than they? And which of you by being anxious can add a single hour to his ... life?"

Day 1

Mission Insight

Jesus' words strike at the deceit of worry, reminding us that God's care is detailed, daily, and ultimately assured. Uniformed service members often carry an extensive amount of concerns: career evolution, family pressure, financial, health issues, or post-service/mobilization identity. These words from Jesus are gentle but firm, God sees you, trust in him. The God who feeds birds and clothes fields knows your name and will provide for you in this life. So do not be unduly anxious, do not let anxiety and fear rule your life; let God rule your life, as He provides for all things He will also for you.

Personal Inspection

If Jesus tells us not to be anxious, do you trust in Him to take over or does your anxiety take over more?

Prayer
Father, help me hand over my worry and believe that You are already working ahead of me; as you have done for even the smallest of your creation, you will undoubtedly do even more for me.

Day 2

Mission Insight
We often struggle with the shift from being in control to living by faith as we've visited before in previous weeks. In the military, anxiety had its place in a way, it pushed us to be prepared, ready, and accountable. But spiritually, Jesus says, worry cannot add anything good. It steals time, peace, and joy. Trust in God and don't be afraid to let go of control and stop looking ahead with trepidation. A strong faith knows that God's got you, live for him at your core and see where it leads you!

Personal Inspection
What has anxiety cost you lately and what might God be asking you to release?

Prayer
Lord, I have too often let worry take the wheel. Help me step back and trust You to lead and navigate my path and leave anxiety in the rearview replaced by optimism ahead.

Day 3

Mission Insight
Jesus points to birds, in comparison to us, they are a small, fragile common creature of the earth. If God cares for them, how much more does He care for those who bear His image? Veterans who

have or may now feel invisible in civilian life need to change their site picture and see that You are of great value to God. For all of us, know that no medal, rank, or resume can enhance or diminish that you are already greater than you can imagine, because He made you in his own image (Gensis 1:27).

Personal Inspection
Where have you based your value on external things and how can you reclaim your worth in God's eyes?

Prayer
God, remind me that I matter not because of what I have done or what material things I may posses, but because I belong to You and am of You.

Day 4

Mission Insight
Jesus is not dismissing your needs, He is pointing you and your needs, to the Father. The shift from worry to trust begins by recognizing who is ultimately responsible and has the power. Leaders of all levels trained to take charge may need to relearn your Father is on watch, in firm command, and He has a perfect record, let Him lead you.

Personal Inspection
What specific concern today that you have in this moment which you need to shift to God's shoulders?

Prayer
Lord, I name this worry before You today. It is too heavy for me but not for You, let my faith be emboldened in the wisdom of knowing worry adds nothing but belief in you gives everything.

Day 5

Mission Insight
The phrase "do not be anxious" is not a command to shut down emotion, emotions are part of God's blessing, rather it's an invitation to open your grip on anxiety. We discussed before how we may tend to internalize everything and may see worry as a part of vigilance, but Christ knows real strength is in surrender, not striving for control. His ask for us to give all we have and follow Him (Matthew 19:21) means giving our worries and burdens up to Him as well.

Personal Inspection
What would it look like to surrender your anxious thoughts instead of managing them alone and letting Jesus work them for a while?

Prayer
Jesus, teach me to let go, one thought, one anxiety at a time if that is what it takes. Replace my mind and life's unease with trust in You, Your Plan for me, and just let You work.

Day 6

Mission Insight
"Which of you by being anxious can add a single hour…?" We often think worry is productive. But we who have served know wasted energy degrades capabilities and resources, becoming counterproductive. Worrying at best gives you something to do, like spinning your tires in the mud, but it does not get you anywhere. Faith and trust, however, leads to action rooted in confidence in Christ.

Personal Inspection

Where are you spinning your wheels and how could peace move you forward more than panic?

Prayer

God, I don't want to burn out chasing control or never knowing peace. Give me wisdom to know the peace you prove and act knowing that Your will and care for me are assured.

Day 7 After-Action Reflection

This week reminded us that God's care is real and significant, that he will provide for those created in His image. You are seen, valued, and provided for by the same God who feeds sparrows and paints sunsets. Your worth is not based on role or productivity it is based on God's love for his sons and daughters. Anxiety is a heavy load but you are not called to carry it alone, peace is available in the One who knows what you need and knows your tomorrows.

Auxiliary Scriptures

- *1 Peter 5:7* "Cast all your anxieties on Him, because He cares for you."
- *Philippians 4:6–7* "Do not be anxious about anything..."

Prayer

Jesus, I release my anxieties to You. Help me live like someone deeply loved, fully provided for and, protected by Your hands. Teach me to trust when I do not understand or still blind to the future.

Field Note

George Müller, a nineteenth century Christian evangelist and director of orphanages in England, Müller resolved never to ask people for money or support but to bring every need to God in prayer. Over the course of his life, he cared for more than 10,000 orphans, established 117 schools, and provided Christian education for more than 120,000 children, often without having funds available beforehand. On countless occasions, the orphanages ran out of food, only for provisions to arrive at the last moment in the form of milk carts breaking down outside their doors or bakers showing up unprompted. Müller never panicked, never worried about "tomorrow," but consistently pointed to God as the supplier of daily needs. (George Muller Biography 2024) His life story is a remarkable embodiment of Jesus' words in Matthew 6:25–27.

WEEK 39 † STRENGTH IN WEAKNESS

Key Verse: *2 Corinthians 12:7-10 (ESV)*

"...A thorn was given me in the flesh... Three times I pleaded with the Lord... But he said to me, 'My grace is sufficient for you, for my power is made perfect in weakness.'... For when I am weak, then I am strong."

Day 1

Mission Insight

This verse records Paul's raw admission of pain, something persistent that would not go away. God did not remove it, instead, He gave Paul grace. For individuals who carry lasting wounds, be they physical, emotional, or spiritual, Paul's testimony is both honest and hopeful. You may not be free from your "thorn", but you are not forsaken in it. God uses weakness to showcase His strength at the same time keeping us humble and grounded. Grace isn't just forgiveness it is power. It is what keeps you going when nothing else makes sense. In God's kingdom, power starts with surrender.

Personal Inspection

What pain do you carry, what thorn has God not removed no matter how much you have asked?

Prayer

God, I may not understand why You have allowed certain pain to remain, but I trust that Your grace and strength is enough to power through, use even my weakness to exemplify You.

Day 2

Mission Insight

Paul pleaded three times for the thorn to be removed. All of us who've prayed for healing, change, or relief and heard "no" or "not yet" can relate. God is not ignoring you, He hears you, possibly He may be using your pain for deeper purpose and if so, approach this with pride.

Personal Inspection

Where have you been pleading with God and what might He be building in the waiting?

Prayer

Lord, I trust You, even when the answer is not what I hoped for. Shape me through this season and realized the prayer not answered or on my timeline maybe the answer I needed after all.

Day 3

Mission Insight

"My grace is sufficient." The word sufficient means it is enough. Not just to get by, but to thrive. You've been taught to be self-governing and structure minded and this may cause you to struggle to receive grace, but God invites you to stop performing and start receiving; it is always ok to take when it is God doing the giving.

Personal Inspection
What are you trying to earn that God simply wants you to receive, maybe all He's wanting for you to do is say thank you?

Prayer
Jesus, I receive what I cannot earn, grace. Let me learn in my heart that it truly is enough for me today and everyday.

Day 4

Mission Insight
"Power made perfect in weakness." On the surface this may seem oxymoronic to us used to military culture, which prizes strength, control, and dominance. But God's power shows up not in performance of deed but in yielding to Him spiritually. Weakness is not disqualification from a relationship with Christ, it's where He is given the opportunity for grace and true strength to work in you.

Personal Inspection
Where do you feel disqualified and how might that be the very place God wants to work?

Prayer
God, I offer You the places I am weakest. Make Your strength visible there for where I am weak you are strong, use me as a living illustration of what your power can do.

Day 5

Mission Insight
Paul did not say he loved pain. But he rejoiced in what it produced which was dependence on God. Undoubtably service has taught you

to push through pain, yet now you have a different challenge, letting Christ carry what once what we burdened ourselves with needlessly, knowing if we allow it, God will work in our weakness and we will emerge more mightily than ever.

Personal Inspection
What would it look like to stop pushing through and start leaning on someone, namely Jesus?

Prayer
Lord, help me to stop pretending I am fine. I want to live in honest dependence on You, let me confess my pain to you, acknowledge it, and let you work in me to get through it.

Day 6

Mission Insight
"When I am weak, then I am strong." Is not a defeatist sentiment, it is truth. Because when you hit your limit, you meet the limitless God. Those of us who feel like they have run out of strength; there is good news, you're finally in the perfect place for God and his grace to take over and he never wears out.

Personal Inspection
Where have you reached the end of your own strength and how can you invite God's strength in?

Prayer
Jesus, let my limits become just the very beginning of Your power in me may it be a testament to others about your greatness and love.

Day 7 After-Action Reflection

This week reminded us that our scars do not disqualify us they qualify us for grace. You do not have to be invincible to be valuable, God uses broken people to display perfect power. You may not get relief the way you expect but you will get grace, and that is what you most need. God's power does not shine through your strength it radiates from your surrender and his strength.

Auxiliary Scriptures

- *Isaiah 40:29* "He gives strength to the weary..."
- *Philippians 4:13* "I can do all things through Him who strengthens me."

Prayer

Father, let Your grace do what I cannot. Make me strong even in my greatest weaknesses You are always enough, and your enough is sufficient to handle all things.

Field Note

President Franklin D. Roosevelt led the United States through the Great Depression and most of World War II, while confined to a wheelchair for much of his adult life due to childhood polio. Roosevelt carefully managed public appearances, not to hide weakness but to maintain a projection of power and confidence. Behind the scenes, he leaned deeply on perseverance, and faith. His limitations sharpened his empathy and resolve. Though not a preacher, Roosevelt would even lead the nation in prayer like on D-Day. ("FDR's Faith" 2023) His life echoed 2 Corinthians 12:10: "When I am weak, then I am strong." It wasn't the absence of struggle that defined him, it was how he persevered through it.

WEEK 40 † HUMILITY AND WISDOM

Key Verse: *Proverbs 16:18-20 (ESV)*

"Pride goes before destruction, and a haughty spirit before a fall… Whoever gives thought to the word will discover good, and blessed is he who trusts in the Lord."

Day 1

Mission Insight

These verses drive to the core of military and post-military life: pride, honor, and trust. Service members are often praised for strength, leadership, and decisiveness but those very strengths can become blind spots where excessive pride is involved. Proverbs warns that unchecked pride leads to collapse. But trust paired with humility, and an open mind rooted in God's Word leads to blessing and wisdom. No mission succeeds on arrogance or conceit. Victory belongs to those who walk with obedience not just confidence; trust in the word is true strength.

Personal Inspection

What has you pride done to play a part in how you interact positively and negatively in the world?

Prayer
God, keep me from the pride that blinds, give me a spirit willingness to learn, listen, and trust You above myself and let me always be aware of my conceit.

Day 2

Mission Insight
"Pride goes before destruction..." It's not a warning for the weak stature, but for the week in spirit. The military culture promotes pride, and that in and of itself is not a bad thing such as esprit de corps. It is the arrogant pride, the one that says I don't need you God I'm good without you is where the damage is done. Proverbs invites you to spot it early, trade it for humility; before you crash down and hard lessons must be learned.

Personal Inspection
Where has pride crept into your mindset or daily life and what would humility look like instead?

Prayer
Lord, help me catch pride before it crashes anything in my life. Teach me to walk humbly before You and live in the word and not my ego.

Day 3

Mission Insight
"It is better to be of a lowly spirit with the poor..." again humility is not weakness, it's strength without ego. In the military, rank matters, to be self-assured is not a bad thing, however all of it must be tempered by and for the faith in Christ. Remember in God's Kingdom,

the lowly are often the greatest for last will be first and the first will be last (Matthew 20:16). Your value is in your heart and your faith, proven by your works, not by your bank balance.

Personal Inspection
How can you choose humility in how you treat others, regardless of status; would you rather be first in this life or first in the next?

Prayer
Jesus, You served even when You had all authority, even washing the feet of Your disciples. Help me to live by Your example in servant leadership.

Day 4

Mission Insight
"Whoever gives thought to the word will discover good…" In the chaos of transition or recovery, or any time really it's easy to stop reflecting on Christ and compound errors or create unnecessary difficulties. However, Proverbs calls us back to the Word; slow down, think deeply, and let Scripture shape your instincts and your actions; good will surely come of it.

Personal Inspection
When was the last time you seriously reflected on God's Word before action and how did it affect your choices?

Prayer
Father, help me value reflection over reaction. Let Your Word guide my decisions especially as it pertains to the scripture I have reflected on today.

Day 5

Mission Insight

"Blessed is he who trusts in the Lord." Blessed is a word thrown around maybe to nonchalantly; it means more than happy or gifted. It means spiritually grounded, protected, flourishing, and rewarded by the Lord. We all too easily get caught up in life and the craziness that makes up this complex world we inhabit; every day we must pause, reflect, give thanks and be grateful because yes, you are truly blessed if you have God in your heart.

Personal Inspection

Where are you still trusting anything but God, what is one thing in your life you can look at or think on that makes you realize how blessed you are and you need to thank God for it?

Prayer

God, I let go of control and open my hands in trust. Be the source of every step I take and let me be aware and cognizant of how you have blessed me in the faith; for these things I am grateful.

Day 6

Mission Insight

These verses link humility, wisdom, and blessing. It is not a checklist I want you to write it is a lifestyle, a culture we must exemplify. If you find yourself navigating reinvention or healing you can embrace this path: humble reflection, honest self-assessment, and trust in your Lord and Savior that leads to transformation and a life of blessing.

Personal Inspection

What does it look like for you to live humbly but confidently in this season of your life, is priority proving yourself to the world or to God?

Prayer

Lord, shape me into someone who leads with quiet strength and walks in faithful trust, let me not be prideful, but do my best to mirror how Jesus lived.

Day 7 After-Action Reflection

This week reminded us that pride can be a quiet or loud enemy; either leading to a fall; yet in contrast humility is a powerful ally. Your strength does not have to come from selfishness or arbitrary titles it can come from relinquished control. God's Word offers a better path than you could ever take on your own, trust in Him fully. You have not been forgotten and those who trust in the Word are and will be blessed.

Auxiliary Scriptures

- *Micah 6:8* "Walk humbly with your God."
- *James 4:6* "God opposes the proud but gives grace to the humble."

Prayer

God, let the pride I possess be in you, let humility shape my heart, wisdom guide my thoughts, and trust in You the creator of heaven and earth, carry my path forward.

Field Note

Nelson Mandela, the former President of South Africa and a key leader in the struggle against apartheid, exemplified humility, wisdom, and belief in something greater than personal ambition. After 27 years in prison, Mandela emerged as a purveyor of peace and unity. ("Nelson Mandela - Biography" 2019) Though quiet about his Christian faith when offered power, he used it not to dominate but to heal, reflective of his beliefs. (Shelton, n.d.) Mandela's life testifies to Proverbs 16:18–20: at a personal cost he lived very humbly, avoided pride's downfall and chose the path of servant leadership, emerging triumphant.

WEEK 41 † STRENGTH IN EVERY CIRCUMSTANCE

Key Verse: *Philippians 4:12-13 (ESV)*

"I know how to be brought low, and I know how to abound… I have learned the secret of facing plenty and hunger, abundance and need. I can do all things through him who strengthens me."

Day 1

Mission Insight

Paul speaks as someone who has seen both sides of life, prosperity and poverty, victory and hardship. In service we often live between those extremes too: the intensity of service followed by the quiet of transition or returning home, the honor of leadership followed by the humility of retirement or relinquishing command. Paul reveals the key to surviving both, Christ's strength. This isn't about positive thinking or pushing through It's about dependency on the One who never quits and cannot be exhausted. Christ does not just help us through adversity, He sustains us in every kind of moment, good or bad.

Personal Inspection

What highs and lows have you encountered, have you been brought through both and stronger now for it?

Prayer
Jesus, I want to know this proclaimed truth from your apostle that lived it, teach me how to walk through both blessing and burden with Your strength alone.

Day 2

Mission Insight
Paul learned the secret, for him it was developed by Jesus over time with a mighty push to get him started while on the road to Damascus. The life of a veteran is much the same, we often face a variety of adversities over time and continue to even after service. What Paul is telling you is that no matter what we face or have faced it all can be conquered by God and in Him we will find the strength we need to overcome.

Personal Inspection
What has hardships in life taught you about God's ability to carry you, and give you confidence in His ability to continue doing so?

Prayer
God, thank You for what You've taught me through difficulty. Help me rely more on You than on myself when I need to find strength to persevere.

Day 3

Mission Insight
"To be brought low" and "to abound" both test our character. Veterans who miss the adrenaline of a high stress life may struggle in quieter seasons. Paul reminds us your worth does not change with

your pace or position. Christ gives strength in both, it is just as easy to stray in both good and bad times; Christ keeps us even keel no matter how smooth or choppy the seas.

Personal Inspection
What season are you in right now abundance or lacking and have you noticed how God is sustaining you through it?

Prayer
Jesus, whether I am standing tall or barely standing, strengthen me today to live faithfully.

Day 4

Mission Insight
Today's service members are expected to be able to do all things, we were often our nation's easy button to respond to a myriad of emergencies and expected to cope. However, Paul redefines the source of our abilities to rise to each occasion and do so successfully, as it pertains to our own wellbeing and heart. Resilience to overcome all things is through Christ, in Him we can do all things.

Personal Inspection
Where are you still relying on your own ways as you approach each day and how can you let Christ strengthen your approach?

Prayer
Lord, I lay down my need to prove something on my own, be my power today especially where I feel weak for I can do all things through Him who strengthens me.

Day 5

Mission Insight

This verse is not about chasing ambition, though there is nothing wrong with that, it's about enduring any and everything. "I can do all things" means you can survive the silence after service, the search for purpose, or temptations in times of abundance; Christ strengthens you not just to fight but to stay faithful in all life's seasons.

Personal Inspection

What season are you tempted to escape instead of enduring and how might Christ strengthen you in it; can you admit to yourself with Him it will be better than on your own?

Prayer

God, help me stay rooted when I want to run never surrendering to life only to You; strengthen me to be present, faithful, and enduring through all periods of life.

Day 6

Mission Insight

Christ does not just strengthen your body He strengthens your heart, soul, and mind. We may still look and give off an aura of strength on the outside, yet still feel hollow within. This verse speaks to that as well; even when you're emotionally empty, Jesus provides internal strength for that too. If your go to is strength but you aren't feeling it on the inside, don't hide it from Jesus, bring it to Him, pray and believe.

Personal Inspection

What's draining you right now and where do you need inner strength, not just outer stamina?

Prayer

Jesus, fill the places in me that feel tired, unseen, or dried out. Be my source of endurance and fulfillment, let us humble the warrior mindset to be bold enough to seek your help.

Day 7 After-Action Reflection

This week reminded us that life happens; good, bad, so-so, etc., you can be at the pinnacle or at the bottom both will be true at some point. You can try and be strong on your own and flounder or you can be strong in anything and everything simply and easily because you allowed Christ to be strong in you. You've been told or have told others, you can do anything you set your mind to, and be whatever you want to be; but in case you did not know how you achieve that, it's through Jesus.

Auxiliary Scriptures

- *Isaiah 40:31* "They shall run and not grow weary..."
- *2 Corinthians 4:16* "Though our outer self is wasting away, our inner self is being renewed..."

Prayer

Lord, thank You for being my strength. In every time and every situation or circumstance, help me to stay solid and steadfast in You.

Field Note

Harriet Tubman, born into slavery and later the leader of the Underground Railroad, she repeatedly risked her life to free the enslaved and her family. She faced immense danger, battled narcolepsy, and had a bounty on her head, yet it did not stop her from making about 13 trips. Nicknamed "Moses," a woman of faith and courage freed 70 slaves from bondage. (National Park Service 2017)

Her life mirrors Philippians 4:13, not just self-reliant, but courage drawn from a deeper source in faith and doing what she believed was right; she knew hardship, but she also knew victory of cause through Christ.

WEEK 42 † COMPASSION & DIVINE PROTECTION

Key Verse: *Psalm 41:1-2 (ESV)*

"Blessed is the one who considers the poor! In the day of trouble the Lord delivers him; the Lord protects him and keeps him alive; he is called blessed in the land; you do not give him up to the will of his enemies."

Day 1

Mission Insight

This psalm opens with a counter cultural promise; God watches over those who watch over others. Those associated with the military often understand what it means to look out for the vulnerable, stand up for those who are oppressed. Psalm 41 affirms that God honors compassion with protection, not as a transaction, but as a reflection of His heart. When we live with mercy, we invite the covering of the Merciful One. The world may overlook the quiet acts of kindness but heaven does not.

Personal Inspection

What do you think of when you read "poor", how might you fit into this category or others close to you?

Prayer

Lord, grow in me a heart of compassion. Help me live and lead others in such a way that honors Your care for the vulnerable, the ones who are poor not just in wealth but in spirit as well.

Day 2

Mission Insight

"Blessed is the one who considers the poor..." The Hebrew root implies thoughtful, intentional care, not pity, as well as an active presence. Caring for others in crisis is part of who we've been trained and taught to be in service, as well as by our faith; a choice we made when we gave our life to God and to our Country. That choice invites blessing from a God who sees what you've done in service, never let your heart be hardened in a way that you stop caring for others.

Personal Inspection

Who around you needs compassion and how can you be present for them this week?

Prayer

God, show me the needs I have been overlooking. Give me eyes like Yours and see this world through your lense, and for the opportunity to do good works today.

Day 3

Mission Insight

"In the day of trouble..." That is when God delivers. When or where is there not trouble in this world? It happens daily and we have our turn like everyone else, sometimes our prior service brings troubles of its own, either in the here and now, or delayed. God tells us that if we are of good heart and do well by others, that in times of trouble he will see that we are not given up to the enemy we face, but will be delivered up by Him.

Personal Inspection
Have you seen God deliver you in seasons of trouble and could it be connected to how you have served others. Is God rewarding you with the same compassion you have shown others?

Prayer
Lord, thank You for remembering me in my times of need, help me trust that mercy echoes and the seeds of goodness I planted will harvest in good will later.

Day 4

Mission Insight
"He is called blessed in the land…" This blessing is public, not hidden. Individuals who have quietly served behind the scenes may one day be honored in ways they never expected. God's economy honors a humble integrity more than those seeking the limelight. Do right, be blessed by the Lord, and seek his glory before your own, and your rewards will be great now and in heaven.

Personal Inspection
What does it mean for you to live a "blessed" life is it one that reflects God's heart and his values, not just worldly success?

Prayer
Jesus, I want to be known for mercy and compassion not titles and medals. Let my legacy reflect Your love over the things that will be forgotten to time or succumb rust.

Day 5

Mission Insight

"You do not give him up to the will of his enemies." God is your defender He will leave no soldier in Christ behind. We who are familiar with the Code of Conduct who have lived under threat may find confidence here as they think of the spiritual threat before them; those who live mercifully are under divine protection and will never be left behind. You are never without an Advocate or a Redeemer when you are doing the right things as God commanded.

Personal Inspection

What enemy external or internal do you need God to defend you from right now? Knowing God will never leave you behind, how does knowing that give you confidence in the fight?

Prayer

Father, stand between me and every enemy seen and unseen I that I must take on; be my confidence as you serve as shield and sword today in this fight against evil.

Day 6

Mission Insight

This verse doesn't glorify suffering rather it honors and inspires compassion. Even those who have served honorably may never feel fully repaid by systems or structures for all they have done and sacrificed, but God promises care that surpasses promotion or benefits. He keeps you alive, body and soul and will ensure you are rewarded for all the good and faithful works you have done for his glory.

Personal Inspection

Where have you been looking for validation that only God can truly provide?

Prayer

Lord thank you that You see what others may have missed. Let me not seek out the kudos of this world as motivation but let Your approval be what focuses and drives me in my actions.

Day 7 After-Action Reflection

This week reminded us that God notices the quiet, compassionate ones and He delivers them in their time of need. I assure you that your mercy has not gone unseen. Whether it was tending to the wounded, saving the oppressed, giving up sleep for a mission, or serving at home God remembers. And He protects those who reflect His heart. In a world where being the loudest is substituted for true strength; though mercy may speak more softly, its impacts are bigger and last longer.

Auxiliary Scriptures

- *Proverbs 19:17* "Whoever is generous to the poor lends to the Lord…"
- *Matthew 5:7* "Blessed are the merciful, for they shall receive mercy."

Prayer

God, let compassion that is reflective of You be my character, help me care and may I rest in the promise that You will care for me in return.

Field Note

Saint Mother Teresa, a personal favorite of mine, lived a life of radical compassion in conditions few would endure voluntarily. Serving the poor, the dying, and destitute in the streets of Calcutta, though of small stature she moved with absolute spiritual power; offering dignity where the world offered none. Her work earned her a Nobel Peace Prize, her life earned her sainthood, yet undoubtably her real reward awaited her in heaven. (Vatican, n.d.) Mother Teresa wholly embodied Psalm 41:1–2, serving as an example and an inspiration to all of the world!

WEEK 43 † THE BEATITUDES

Key Verse: *Matthew 5:2-12 (ESV)*

"Blessed are the poor in spirit, for theirs is the kingdom of heaven. Blessed are those who mourn, for they will be comforted. Blessed are the meek, for they will inherit the earth. Blessed are those who hunger and thirst for righteousness, for they will be filled. Blessed are the merciful, for they will be shown mercy. Blessed are the pure in heart, for they will see God. Blessed are the peacemakers, for they will be called children of God. Blessed are those who are persecuted because of righteousness, for thiers is the kingdom of heaven. Blessed are you when people insult you, persecute you and falsely say all kins of evil against you because of me. Rejoice and be glad, because great is your reward in heaven..."

Day 1

Mission Insight

Jesus taught these during His Sermon on the Mount and they were too important to summarize. At the time He said these words they would have been culturally uncommon teachings on how to live as a child of God. These were revolutionary, a new way of being; the weak are strong, the grieving are comforted, the lowly are lifted. etc. Military members trained to follow structure, use force as a means, may find these to be contrarian to the service they executed. They show us what *it means to live in Christ*: merciful, humble, peacemaking, pure of heart, bold in faith, courageous in persecution. These are not what armies are built on, yet has allowed Christianity to permeate every corner of the Earth.

Personal Inspection

What in how you live is reflective of how bold Jesus' words were for the time he delivered this message?

Prayer

Jesus, help me value what You value. Let these Kingdom qualities become part of who I am, not let them just be hollow platitudes or just what I admire, but what I truly emulate in my life.

Day 2

Mission Insight

"Blessed are the poor in spirit…" That means those who know they need God. We as people often struggle with asking for help physically or spiritually or think we know what is best for ourselves. But here is the covenant with Jesus, even those who come empty-handed with nothing more than a belief in Jesus can be saved and blessed. God knows what we need, and it's Him first.

Personal Inspection

Have you given yourself to God, did you know you were spiritually devoid without Him, are you still holding back or all it?

Prayer

Lord, I do not have it all together, and I do not always know what I need; let me always turn to you with sincere belief Your ability to guide me and lead me to the Kingdom.

Day 3

Mission Insight

"Blessed are those who mourn..." Jesus does not ask you to suppress grief, it's a part of life He promises to meet you in it and bring you comfort. Does not mater military or civilian, loss and mourning are something we will encounter, when it happens go to Him and you will find comfort and peace.

Personal Inspection

Where have you grieved without thinking of Jesus, heaven, and eternal life, how might God be inviting you to receive His comfort?

Prayer

Father, I give You my sorrow. Comfort me through this with the true perspective that Your grace gifted us eternal life, and though we sorrow today joy awaits all who believe in You.

Day 4

Mission Insight

Like we discussed in Mathew 5:9 "Blessed are the peacemakers..." Not the peacekeepers, the peacemakers. That is hard, sacrificial work. Service members of warzones or who have been to areas of conflict may feel disillusioned about peace, but Jesus honors those who build it, brick by painful brick.

Personal Inspection

Where are you being called to create peace in your home, community, or past this week?

Prayer

God, make me a builder of peace not a reactor to chaos or someone watching from the sidelines, engage me to be active and the courage to endure the challenge.

Day 5

Mission Insight

"Blessed are the merciful..." Mercy and forgiveness are a powerful unsung force of justice, it liberates both the giver and the receiver. God blesses those who let go of bitterness and extend grace. Does not mean there should not be accountability or justice done, but where the heart is pure on either end of a conflict, let there be love expressed for each other's humanity.

Personal Inspection

Who do you need to show mercy and forgiveness to, possibly including yourself?

Prayer

Jesus, teach me to forgive like You. Let mercy shape how I treat others and even myself.

Day 6

Mission Insight

"Blessed are those who are persecuted..." Persecution happens to us all, at varying degrees some more than others, but to be persecuted on behalf of Jesus or to handle any persecution the righteous way, He tells us as a result yours will be the kingdom of heaven. It will still sting, but we can rejoice and numb the pain knowing we are doing right, and are pleasing to God in our actions.

Personal Inspection

Have you felt alone for doing what is right and how can you take comfort in this promise?

Prayer

Lord, give me courage to keep doing what is right over taking the easy wrongs in life, even when it's costly.

Day 7 After-Action Reflection

This week showed us what the Kingdom of God values and how those values often clash with the world's cultural ones. God's blessing rests not on power or pride but on humility, mercy, and strength. Knowing this consider your mission may now be more about character than ever before. The Beatitudes remind us God's reward is real and your inheritance in heaven is secure.

Auxiliary Scriptures

- *Micah 6:8* "Do justice, love mercy, and walk humbly..."
- *Romans 12:21* "Do not be overcome by evil, but overcome evil with good."

Prayer

Jesus, help me represent Your kingdom even when the world misunderstands it. Shape me to reflect Your values living for heaven's eternal reward, not the tarnishing rewards of this world.

Field Note

Dietrich Bonhoeffer, a German theologian and pastor, openly resisted the Nazi regime during World War II. He helped form underground seminaries and boldly served the resistance in Germany despite an order by the Nazis forbidding him from public speaking.

Arrested and later executed as a conspirator for trying to rescue Jews, (United States Holocaust Memorial Museum, Washington, DC 2009) Bonhoeffer lived out his life in the strong belief of Jesus' teaching in Matthew 5:2–12 and active discipleship in giving voice to the word.

WEEK 44 † GRACE FOR THE HUMBLE

Key Verse: *James 4:6-8 (ESV)*

"… God opposes the proud but gives grace to the humble. Submit yourselves therefore to God. Resist the devil… Draw near to God, and he will draw near to you."

Day 1

Mission Insight

James offers a battle-ready spiritual sequence: humility, submission, resistance, nearness. All service members understand structure and value systems, this passage offers a similar kind of spiritual clarity and that is serving God. He gives grace, not to the proud but to the humble. He opposes pride, not because He dislikes confidence, but because pride shuts the door to grace and opens to the door to the devil. To accept the One is to come under His command and to fight evil wearing the armor of God. And the reward is, that God draws near, and all the good that comes with that.

Personal Inspection

What about your experience has kept you from accepting humility or being more humble in the future?

Prayer

Lord, help me lay down my foolish prides I've learned in my life. Let me rather submit to Your ways, resist what would destroy me, and walk into deeper relationship with You.

Day 2

Mission Insight

God doesn't tell us not to have pride in ourselves or what we have done but to be proud and humble. We are achieved by his Grace, and failure to recognize the source of our success is like forgetting to thank your Mom for being born. He will give unending grace to the humble because it means that you are able to come to Him and away from the dictation of the world or the influence of the evil one. His grace is far greater than all the atta-boys you can give yourself.

Personal Inspection

Where have you been assuming all the credit and exerting selfish pride in your life?

Prayer

God, I have felt at times like I have greater power and control than I really do, let me accept your power in humility and the peace that comes from You being in ultimate control.

Day 3

Mission Insight

"God opposes the proud…" This strong language is similar to week 40. Selfish pride is not a bad habit it's spiritual rebellion against God. Trained to act with confidence and embrace unit pride you may possibly struggle to distinguish pride that is rebellious and that which can be positive. But the line is this, a rebellious pride serves self. A humble heart is the cure to this problem, and ironically the more humble you are, the greater your life, and the more you'll have to be proud of.

Personal Inspection

Where is pride keeping you from receiving grace how is lack of humility holding you back?

Prayer

Father, reveal pride in me even if the truth is hard to bare. Help me trade control for surrender and independence for intimacy with You.

Day 4

Mission Insight

"Submit yourselves… Resist the devil…" The order matters. Before resistance comes submission, much like before service comes the decision to sign up. Warriors who fight well must first know who they fight for and with, and join a service, a unit, or a team. You can't fight evil on your own terms you need alignment with God's mission and be part of His service.

Personal Inspection

Are you trying to resist temptation or evil without first submitting to God, is it going well?

Prayer

Lord, I choose to come under Your command. Teach me to not resist alone, but gain strength and power in this spiritual battle by alignment with You, so that I may be delivered from every evil.

Day 5

Mission Insight

"Draw near to God, and he will draw near to you." This theme reoccurs throughout the New Testament, and that's because God gives you the choice to accept and be in Him. When you do, He is there ready and will be near, always! Anyone exposed to the military life through that lifestyle or its learned behaviors may experience spiritual drift and feel distant from God. However, he tells you, that it's only in your mind that you are distant, he is actually still near, and ever the closer you get to Him, He comes closer. It's your choice to make, He has already decided to choose you.

Personal Inspection

What is one step you can take today to draw near to God, big or small?

Prayer

Jesus, I am turning toward You. Meet me in this moment You promised You would and it is in your promise I find a reassuring confidence that you will receive me.

Day 6

Mission Insight

This passage is a roadmap for spiritual realignment. If you are facing inner battles, external pressures, feelings of hopelessness, or being alone and forgotten you can come back to this; grace > pride, submission > rebellion, proximity > distance. You don't have to figure it all out just follow the steps and let God work in your life to address your concerns, and if you're humble enough to receive Him, He will come through for you as He will be right there with you the whole way.

Personal Inspection
What part of this sequence grace, humility, submission, resistance to evil, or nearness do you need most right now?

Prayer
Lord, guide me step by step, let Your grace cover my weakness and develop in me where I need it most at this stage of my journey with You.

Day 7 After-Action Reflection

This week reminded us that spiritual life is not ambiguous; God gives us a playbook. God gives grace when we are humble, strength when we submit to him, helps us resist evil, and brings closeness to the seeking. You have fought hard in other ways now fight under God's instruction. You do not have to earn God's favor, you just need to receive it, submit to it, and walk in it. Remember when you draw near to Him, He does not hesitate He moves forward to be near to you!

Auxiliary Scriptures

- *1 Peter 5:6–9* "Humble yourselves… resist the devil…"
- *Psalm 145:18* "The Lord is near to all who call on him…"

Prayer
God, I am ready to be inwardly selfless, submit to Your will. resist evil. and seek You. Let Your grace meet me where I am and shape me into who You have called me to be.

Field Note

King Alfred the Great, constantly under assault from the Danes, became king of Wessex at the age of 21 when his brother died. Pushed back, and forced into guerrilla warfare, the King continued to fight the Danes until successfully defeating them at the battle of Edington. This led to a peace treaty with the Dane leader King Guthrum. Guthrum later converted to Christianity and chose King Alfred as his Godfather. (Ciara Berry 2016) The King resembled James 4:6–8; his humble, persistent, and resilient spirit, was rewarded with God's nearness and peace.

WEEK 45 † SELF-EXAMINATION BEFORE CORRECTION

Key Verse: *Luke 6:41-42 (ESV)*

"Why do you see the speck that is in your brother's eye, but do not notice the log that is in your own eye?... First take the log out of your own eye, and then you will see clearly..."

Day 1

Mission Insight
Jesus confronts the human tendency toward hypocrisy seeing the flaws of others over our own. You are accustomed to discipline, standards, and good order which may mean you sometimes default to correcting others whether in the home, workplace, or church. Jesus tells us to meet our own standards first, before criticizing others. He is not saying ignore wrongdoing, He is saying start with yourself! When we begin with self-awareness instead of blame, we become a more effective, compassionate, and credible leader and Christian. True transformation flows outward only after it begins inward.

Personal Inspection
What about self-honesty is difficult, is being honest with yourself being honest with God also?

Prayer
God, help me be honest with myself before I try to correct anyone else, teach me to lead with humility and self-awareness rather than hypocrisy and finger pointing.

Day 2

Mission Insight
Jesus uses the exaggerated image of a log in your eye to emphasize how obvious our own faults can be yet how blind we are to them. Veterans who have led others know the importance of clear vision to be able to evaluate others and train to standard. Spiritually, that means you must be the standard bearer first before addressing other's shortcomings… i.e. lead by example!

Personal Inspection
Where are you most tempted to focus on others' faults before examining your own?

Prayer
Lord, open my eyes first to my own heart and my own business, so I can then see others more clearly and compassionately in the same grace which You see me.

Day 3

Mission Insight
"Then you will see clearly…" Self-examination isn't about shame, though it is hard to do at times, rather it is about clarity. I know you are familiar with debriefs and after-action reviews, so you know the value of an honest assessment. The same applies to spiritual growth; correction begins with truthful candor about ourselves, who we really are, and what we can do to improve.

Self-Reflection;
What's one "log" in your life you have been ignoring willfully and what's your next step toward addressing it, isn't it time?

Prayer
Jesus, give me courage to see, to face, and take action on what needs to change in me.

Day 4

Mission Insight
Jesus never says do not help your brother or stand up against the wrongs of the world. He says help him after you've looked inward. Anyone in leadership or mentorship roles must model that order; start with integrity, then correct with grace, that's how real respect is earned, and it's exactly how Christ has led.

Personal Inspection
Who are you trying to help right now and how could personal honesty make your influence more effective?

Prayer
God, let my help come from a place of humility, not hypocrisy, let me understand that I must accept my reality of who I am while working to right the wrongs around me.

Day 5

Mission Insight
This passage reminds us that accountability begins with ourselves. So common sense you would think but a large blind spot for many of us. Those of us who know what it is like to hold a standard must

remember that God's standard begins with the heart, and that where our first inspection should be. Change what we see in the mirror before pointing out the window.

Personal Inspection
What is one area where your actions need to better align with your expectations of others?

Prayer
Father, let me pursue a life of integrity and be honest in my self-assessments to drive self-improvement with your grace and guidance, so that I may help others find your guiding light.

Day 6

Mission Insight
Correcting others is part of leadership, but it must be done thoughtfully and with credibility. I don't' mean to lecture, however, leaders who are respected most often are not the loudest, but the most honest. We all know those leaders who are do as I say not as I do examples. Jesus was a leader that did all that he has asked us to do and more; he showed us how to not only live but how to lead as well.

Personal Inspection
What kind of voice do you want to be in someone's life, a hypocrite or a shining example?

Prayer
Jesus, shape my tone to match the lessons You taught, and done in the example you set.

Day 7 After-Action Reflection

This week reminded us that good leadership and strong relationships begin with honest self-assessment. Your strength to improve in your faith lies not in flawless performance but in courageous introspection. The world does not need more critics it needs more Christlike examples. When you own your flaws and lead with humility, you help others do the same.

Auxiliary Scriptures

- *Galatians 6:1* "Restore him in a spirit of gentleness..."
- *Proverbs 27:6* "Faithful are the wounds of a friend..."

Prayer

God, help me see myself clearly not to feel shame, but to grow in grace. Let my life lead others closer to You from a place of integrity and being a Christlike example.

Field Note

President Harry S. Truman, often remembered for dropping the bombs on Japan to end WWII, was also known for his motto, "The buck stops here." His philosophy was that he was The President; he was in charge and he had to make decisions and own them. He believed in taking responsibility, looking at himself for the cause of his successes and failures, rather than looking for others to blame or scapegoats when things went wrong. (Joyce 2020) This belief system exemplifies what we find in Luke 6:41–42: he believed in personal accountability and introspection before looking for ways to blame or find fault in others.

WEEK 46 † LIVING WATER

Key Verse: *John 4:13-14 (ESV)*

"Jesus said to her, 'Everyone who drinks of this water will be thirsty again, but whoever drinks of the water that I will give him will never be thirsty again. The water that I will give him will become in him a spring of water welling up to eternal life.'"

Day 1

Mission Insight
Jesus speaks these words to a Samaritan woman, a social outcast looking for worth, love, and meaning, in all the wrong places. Those of us who have served may know what it's like to chase satisfaction in empty places; promotion, distraction, adrenaline, titles; I too was enticed by these from time to time. Jesus offers something better, living water. Not a temporary fix, but an eternal wellspring of purpose, identity, and peace. The things of this world always leave us thirsty again, they have no stay. But when we come to Jesus, He fills us with something that endures forever without tarnish, and transforms us from the inside out.

Personal Inspection
What is it you tried to quench your thirst with that did not work, are you still thirsty?

Prayer
Jesus, I've chased many things that did not satisfy me thought I thought they would. Today I turn to You for the water that truly gives life so that I truly may feel quenched.

Day 2

Mission Insight
"Everyone who drinks this water will be thirsty again…" This world offers many short-term "fixes" that never truly satisfy. People coming out of high-tempo environments may turn to habits that offer relief, not restoration. But Jesus sees through the unproductive cycle we may choose for ourselves to cope, and offers real change that will endure any season of your life; He gives it, all you must do is drink.

Personal Inspection
What temporary things have you been turning to for peace, and what would it look like to turn to Jesus instead?

Prayer
Lord, break the counterproductive cycle I have been leading, lead me away from what does not truly bring any real satisfaction or purpose and bring me back to You.

Day 3

Mission Insight
"Living water." This is not just sentimental greeting card gesture it is a metaphor for who and what Jesus is. Jesus offers His Spirit, His presence, and His peace. Those of us "living the dream" or have gotten a bit "crusty" dealing with a drought of motivation, burnout, or spiritual numbness need to know the following. He does not just

restore, He replenishes; unlike water from a well, drink living water once and you are refreshed forever, because that is what belief in Jesus will do for you.

Personal Inspection
Where do you feel spiritually dry and how can you invite Jesus to refill that part of your life?

Prayer
Jesus, breathe life back into the dry places flood them with Your spirit. Let Your presence be my wellspring today.

Day 4

Mission Insight
"...a spring of water welling up..." What Christ gives doesn't stay stagnant, it overflows it is meant to bubble up and flow outward from you. Men and women shaped by service know the importance of pouring into others such as, time, effort, blood, sweat, tears, and treasure. Jesus has done just this for you so that you become a source of hope for those around you not just tangibly, but spiritually.

Personal Inspection
Who around you needs the overflow of your spiritual life and what's one way you can pour out what Jesus has put into you, into them?

Prayer
God, let me receive Your life, Your sacrifice, and Your spirit deeply and share it freely. Make me a spring for others, not only a reservoir for myself.

Day 5

Mission Insight

Jesus met the Samaritan woman at a well and He meets you in ordinary places too. People in life's seasonal transitions, in pain, or just in need, can find Him right where they are, there is literally no place that Jesus can't go. You do not have to "go" anywhere to encounter living water, just bring your thirst.

Personal Inspection

Where is Jesus meeting you in your daily life and how is He inviting you to drink deeply?

Prayer

Lord, thank You for showing up in my ordinary moments and for letting me know at any time and any place I can reach out and You will be there. Teach me to drink from Your grace daily.

Day 6

Mission Insight

"...eternal life." Maybe you are used to planning in the short-term for missions or even a couple of years out be it for deployments, construction projects, or purchasing contracts. But when we plan and when we focus its usually for just a set timeframe. Jesus offers a forever promise. Living water means life that begins now and never ends, it's all part of being born again, a promise of an everlasting tomorrow. If it is important to plan for the short-term is it not even more important to plan for eternity with Jesus and give that spiritual part of our future even more attention?

Personal Inspection

How does knowing your soul is eternally secure by His grace change how you live right now?

Prayer

Jesus, thank You that my life is not limited to what I see or the clock on the wall. Help me live with eternity in mind and may it reflect in how I live and prioritize my life.

Day 7 After-Action Reflection

This week reminded us that Christ is the only source of lasting satisfaction. Sorry, no social media, no bottle, no bar, no hoping beds, is going to do the same. Those of us who have searched for identity or peace in worldly things can find a better way, Jesus Christ, His living water. It does not just quench the moment, it is not temporary, it changes you forever. You do not have to stay thirsty, you do not have to stay empty. He invites you to drink deeply, live fully, and let that new life overflow into the world around you.

Auxiliary Scriptures

- *Isaiah 55:1–2* "Come, everyone who thirsts… why do you spend money for that which does not satisfy?"
- *Revelation 21:6* "To the thirsty I will give from the spring of the water of life without payment."

Prayer

Jesus, You are the only One that can truly satisfy our soul and bring fulness to our lives. Fill me, change me, and make me part of Your grace to others as I overflow exemplifying Your truth.

Field Note

Saint Longinus, is the Roman centurion who is traditionally identified as the soldier who oversaw Jesus' crucifixion and pierced Jesus' side with a spear. (John 19:34) Early Christian tradition tells us that he underwent a radical transformation after witnessing Christ's death. When he saw how Jesus died, he proclaimed "Truly this was the Son of God." (Mark 15:39) Early accounts say he converted, left the military, lived as a Christian, and proclaimed publicly about the resurrection and was later martyred for his faith. (Fr. Stavros Akrotirianakis 2024) Longinus's story reflects John 4:13–14: having previously been a man of sin of the worst kinds, it proves no one is too far gone for redemption; he turned to the only source of eternal life, the living water Christ provides.

WEEK 47 † FIGHT THE GOOD FIGHT

Key Verse: *1 Timothy 6:10-12 (ESV)*

> **"For the love of money is a root of all kinds of evils... But as for you, ... flee these things. Pursue righteousness, godliness, faith, love, steadfastness, gentleness. Fight the good fight of the faith..."**

Day 1

Mission Insight

Paul warns Timothy about misplaced priorities, especially the dangers of wealth or material obsession. All of us in general no matter where we come from may encounter a strong pull toward chasing financial gain, status, or material security. But Scripture calls us to flee from those temptations being our main motivation, not because success is wrong, but because misplaced devotion can slowly erode our soul. Instead, we are invited to pursue something with greater priority which Paul lists out as righteousness, godliness, faith, love, perseverance, and gentleness. These traits build legacy, strengthen character, reflect Christ. That is the good fight, the one worth showing up for every single day.

Personal Inspection

What do you think about more in a day God and his mission for you or money, what drives you more?

Prayer
Lord, train my heart to pursue what lasts. Help me flee distraction and fight the good fight of faith and not compromise myself for wealth or succumb to evil ways.

Day 2

Mission Insight
"For the love of money…" Money and wealth itself isn't evil it's the love of it that entangles mankind, much like the Spanish Conquistadors in the 1500s. Those seeking stability can be vulnerable to chasing wealth instead of purpose, this verse refocuses us to seek God, not gold.

Personal Inspection
Where have your priorities been drifting towards material wealth more than God and what would realignment toward godliness look like?

Prayer
Jesus, You are priceless and the true treasure of my life, keep me from chasing what fades and in turn, missing what lasts.

Day 3

Mission Insight
"Flee these things…" These words make up a commanding phrase. It is not solely about resisting greed, it is about running from it. You are used to engaging and running towards threats however it is the opposite spiritually; not only are we to flee from them directly but also not align our lives with those who embody the things we are trying to escape from.

Personal Inspection

What unhealthy pursuit or environment do you need to walk (or run) away from right now?

Prayer

God, show me the exits, you have put them in bright lights yet so many miss them. Give me strength to leave behind what pulls me from You.

Day 4

Mission Insight

"Pursue righteousness, godliness, faith…" You are familiar with having a mission focus, Jesus calls you to a mission, the highest and most important you will ever pursue; one not measured in medals, or your glory, but in spiritual reward and His glory. These mission successes will not trend on social media or the news, but they will truly matter in this life and the next.

Personal Inspection

Which of the six qualities listed (righteousness, godliness, faith, love, steadfastness, gentleness) is God highlighting for your growth today?

Prayer

Lord, help me pursue the virtues that build character and reflect Your heart while rejecting evil.

Day 5

Mission Insight

"Fight the good fight…" Not all fights are worth your energy, God gave us life so that we may pick our battles. Though there is no greater purpose that to fight for and alongside Jesus. We who have trained for or fought hard battles physically or emotionally may be tempted to rest spiritually; However, the fight for integrity, love, and truth never ends. Stay suited up, the uniform of a warrior for Christ is permanently worn, do so proudly and boldly.

Personal Inspection

What fight are you called to keep showing up for and how is God strengthening you in it?

Prayer

God, I do not want to fight aimlessly I want to be justified fighting for what matters. Equip me daily for spiritual warfare and let your victory be my sustaining motivation to never surrender.

Day 6

Mission Insight

Veterans just like everyone else are called to action, to flee temptation, pursue godliness, fight faithfully. You're not just surviving life during or after service you are continuing in service at all times to the Lord shaping it through intentional, Spirit-filled effort. You have the skills Jesus can work through to do great things, let Him.

Personal Inspection

What's one way you can actively pursue the mission of faith this week big or small, simple or complex?

Prayer

Jesus, energize my spirit. Help me live today like it matters eternally and help me prioritize what really matters in this miracle called life that You, have given me.

Day 7 After-Action Reflection

This week reminded us that the battle worth fighting is internal, spiritual, against selfishness, distractions, discontentment, and misplace priorities. You have trained to face the physical enemy one you can see and engage with. Now God calls you to face spiritual ones, those that cannot be defeated with weapons but rather with His armor and His weaponry. The call is clear, flee what corrupts, pursue what is holy, and fight the good fight. It is not easy but it is worth it and the rewards are great!

Auxiliary Scriptures

- *2 Timothy 4:7* "I have fought the good fight, I have finished the race..."
- *Matthew 6:33* "Seek first the kingdom of God..."

Prayer

Father, fix my eyes on the right fight. Make me bold in fleeing evil, faithful in pursuit of godliness, and steady in the storms should they befall me.

Field Note

General Charles George Gordon, a 19th-century British Army officer who despite his military skill, was deeply committed to living with integrity, courage and righteousness. He fought not just for empire, but for justice, famously opposing the slave trade in Sudan and adopting an abandoned child he found on the battlefield. He cited his faith for his humility and sacrificial leadership believing he was protected at God's will, often going into battle leading his men unarmed. Though ultimately killed during the Siege of Khartoum in 1885 after holding the town for 10 months, Gordon's legacy has endured. (The New York Times 1955) His life echoed 1 Timothy 6:12: He fought the good fight, not for wealth or fame but for righteousness derived from his faith in Christ.

WEEK 48 † ABOUNDING IN HOPE

Key Verse: *Romans 15:13 (ESV)*

> **"May the God of hope fill you with all joy and peace in believing, so that by the power of the Holy Spirit you may abound in hope."**

Day 1

Mission Insight

This verse is a prayer for joy, peace, and especially hope. Ones who have experienced despair or surrendered to disillusionment may struggle to reconnect with hope. But Paul reminds us hope is not arbitrarily manufactured, it's real and ever present, given by God, through the Holy Spirit. When life is challenging, chaotic, or uncertain, the Holy Spirit does not just provide survival through hard times it gives joy, peace, and hope that defies circumstances and helps us to come out better on the other side of any downward season. Those who believe always have hope.

Personal Inspection

When do you simply rejoice alone in the fact that you are blessed and able to believe and live in Christ?

Prayer

God of hope, fill me today. Let Your joy and peace take root in me and produce hope I cannot create on my own.

Day 2

Mission Insight

"The God of hope..." That is part of who He is and what He gives. Veterans whose experiences that have clouded their view of God can read this and now anchor here, knowing He has not abandoned you He is hope, therefore you have Hope. Believe and pray; and you will see you are not alone and have not' been forgotten.

Personal Inspection

How does knowing that God is the God of hope change how you face your current challenges?

Prayer

Father, when I forget who You are, remind me. Let hope rise again in my heart and in my life.

Day 3

Mission Insight

"Fill you with all joy and peace..." Joy and peace don't mean the absence of problems we discussed before how life will have its tribulations, but it does mean stability in the middle of them, we know this also by what we are told and read earlier in John 16:33. If you feel tossed around by emotions, memories, or civilian transition/life steady yourself knowing joy and peace are always available, always possible, and always present, with God in our lives.

Personal Inspection

What is draining your joy or peace and how can you open that for God to fill?

Prayer
Lord, you never said life would be easy or without troubles, but I ask you to let me find joy amid the journey and keep my heart loyal and faithful to You and confident in the hope You give.

Day 4

Mission Insight
"In believing…" Faith is not inert it is the living means by which hope flows. In the service we are trained in our jobs so that we can believe in ourselves to do what is asked of us when the time comes; it is belief in ourselves and abilities that makes us good at our jobs. Much like this, it is our belief in our faith and our ability to accept Jesus that makes room for the Holy Spirit to move mountains in us.

Personal Inspection
What belief do you need to reaffirm in your heart today to keep hope alive?

Prayer
Jesus, strengthen my faith even when it is shaky, help me hold on to Your truth, so that I may know I possess the belief in You and myself to succeed where You have placed me in this life.

Day 5

Mission Insight
"By the power of the Holy Spirit…" The belief in hope and its validity isn't illogical, yet there is no tangible launch button to press, rather it is Spirit-infused and faith powered that provides hope's legitimacy and creation. Anyone struggling trying to "hold it

together" needs this reminder, you do not have to muster your own hope. God supplies it through His Spirit in you, look to Him!

Personal Inspection

Where are you trying to "power through" on your own strength and how can you surrender to the Spirit and in turn be rewarded with true hope?

Prayer

Holy Spirit, I cannot and was never meant to do this alone. Fill me with strength and hope that only You can give me.

Day 6

Mission Insight

"You may abound in hope." Not a trickle. Not a smidge, but rather abound, as in abundance! God wants to fill you to the point of overflow, not just provide the bare minimum. We who have known seasons of scarcity emotionally or spiritually can bank this promise personally; an abundance of hope is truly possible. Never give up, never surrender!

Personal Inspection

What would your life look like if hope were abounding, not just there a little bit, but your perspective of faith provided a true abundance of hope surrounding your life?

Prayer

God, I am done living on an emptiness filled only by pessimism and limited thinking. Fill me with hope that empowers me and touches others, knowing all things are possible through you.

Day 7 After-Action Reflection

This week reminded us that hope is not fleeting it's abundant when fueled by God's Spirit. Whether you are just surviving or seeking to thrive, this promise is yours that the God of hope can fill you today. Not just with momentary encouragement but with lasting peace and joy that produces endurance. Do not settle for a trickle when God offers an abundance; believe, receive, and abound in hope.

Auxiliary Scriptures

- *Isaiah 40:31* "Those who hope in the Lord shall renew their strength..."
- *Lamentations 3:22–23* "The Lord's mercies are new every morning... therefore I will hope in Him."

Prayer

God, thank You for real hope. Let Your Spirit fill me again today. Overflow my life with the joy and peace that comes only from You.

Field Note

President Abraham Lincoln led the United States through its most divided era, the Civil War. Personally afflicted by sorrow, Lincoln battled profound grief after the deaths of his children and carried the burden of preserving the Union while confronting the moral and human toll of slavery and war. Despite these pressures, he maintained a steady public posture of humility, reflection, and deep hope. His speeches and personal letters often referenced Scripture, divine providence, and the pursuit of peace. ("Abraham Lincoln and the Bible – Abraham Lincoln's Classroom" 2025) Lincoln's faith in God's guidance, paired with his enduring pursuit of unity and justice, reflects the spirit of Romans 15:13: a man sustained by sturdy belief, who never gave up hope when the nation needed it most.

WEEK 49 † PRAISING AND WORSHIP

Key Verse: *Hebrews 13:15-16 (ESV)*

"Let us continually offer up a sacrifice of praise to God... Do not neglect to do good and to share what you have, for such sacrifices are pleasing to God."

Day 1

Mission Insight

Worship isn't confined to a church building or music; according to Hebrews a book setting expectations and standards for a new faith, it is something we live out daily by giving thanks, doing good, and sharing what we have. For those of service, this offers a practical model of faith. A "sacrifice of praise" may mean lifting up thanks even in grief, or pain. And doing good? That's often muscle memory for those who've served and adhered to the services values. But God doesn't just want any outward action, He wants hearts rooted in gratefulness and generosity; praise and sacrifice that mean something

Personal Inspection

What of your time, self, or wealth can you give to serve God's will, do you do this enough?

Prayer
Lord, let my life be more than words. Teach me to praise You with action and serve You with a grateful and generous heart.

Day 2

Mission Insight
"Let us continually offer..." That is consistency, not convenience. Service life knows the importance of daily routine or doing that which is not convenient because it is right and has to get done. Spiritually, praising God isn't about feeling when you feel it it's about choosing Him for eternity. That means rain or shine in good and bad that we paise Him, His will is His own, and we may not understand but we must have faith He has a plan and it is truly for our own good.

Personal Inspection
When was the last time you praised God even when it was difficult and what came from that choice?

Prayer
God, give me a heart that can see the bigger picture and that praises You on the hard days, not just the good ones.

Day 3

Mission Insight
"A sacrifice of praise..." As I have said before those who have served know sacrifice better than most; long hours, separation, loss of experiences or time. Praise can feel costly, especially after trauma or disappointment. But Hebrews reminds us, that's the very moment when praise pleases God most. Think about it, do you feel best about

your friends when they are fair weathered or rather when they show their loyalty in the hard and trying times?

Personal Inspection

What pain or hardship could become a place of worship if you surrendered it to God?

Prayer

Jesus, receive my praise even when it comes through tears, let my heart not lose faith but rather reenforced by Your eternal presence and love.

Day 4

Mission Insight

"Do not neglect to do good…" Sometimes we separate worship from action. We sing and pray loudly in the pews and then exit the doors and return to a life of sin and faithlessness. Veterans for example who continue to serve others even when they no longer have to, through mentorship, volunteering, or just showing up in support are living this verse. Worship is more than showing up to Sunday service, it is about showing up every day.

Personal Inspection

Where is God calling you to do good, not just Sunday, not just someday, but today?

Prayer

Lord, open my eyes to someone I can help today. Let my service reflect Your goodness.

Day 5

Mission Insight

"Share what you have..." That may mean money, but it may also mean time, wisdom, or just being engaged and caring in someone's life. You have experiences and perspective others need. Sharing them (and I don't necessarily mean war stories) be it values, testimonials, work ethic, etc., that are reflective of the faith is a form of ministry, one you're amply trained to give.

Personal Inspection

What do you have that someone else needs, and how can you offer it this week?

Prayer

God, let me be generous with all You have given me, my blessings, my story, my time, and my heart.

Day 6

Mission Insight

"For such sacrifices are pleasing to God." God's not looking for flashy or performative sacrifices, just faithful true of heart ones. Familiar with quiet service without needing recognition, you have already modeled this kind of daily offering, by being humble, consistent, and quietly powerful; like traits we often find within the creeds of our Non-Commissioned Officers. This approach to giving who you are for God's purpose are sacrifices He finds pleasing.

Personal Inspection

How can you turn an action into a spiritual offering today while remaining humble?

Prayer
Lord, make my life holy. Help me give You praise in the little things and act with humility.

Day 7 After-Action Reflection

This week reminded us that worship is not just a singular event it is a daily lifestyle. Remember, your praise to God matters even if it is quiet, hesitant, or offered in the middle of struggle; God calls that a sacrifice and it pleases Him. When you serve others, share your life, and keep giving thanks, you are not just doing good, you're worshipping selflessly. That is the kind of offering God never overlooks and will always remember.

Auxiliary Scriptures
- *Romans 12:1* "Offer your bodies as a living sacrifice..."
- *Psalm 34:1* "I will bless the Lord at all times..."

Prayer
Jesus, let my praise rise even when life feels hard. Let my service bring You glory and make my life an offering that pleases You.

Field Note
The Apostle John, an original disciple and the author of the Gospel of John, three epistles and the Book of Revelation, lived a long life of faithful and sacrificial service. Known as "the disciple whom Jesus loved," John was a bold witness, a loving shepherd of early churches, and a prophetic voice. John faced persecution like all the disciples, after a botched execution he was later exiled to the island of Patmos. Due to being the longest living disciple, he watched the persecution of Christians and the

martyrdom of the other disciples; though despite it all he never ceased to offer the Lord praise. John urged believers to love not just in word but also in deed. (Crossway Bibles 2016) Echoing Hebrews 13:16: do not neglect to do good, share what you have, and give Him praise.

WEEK 50 † THE WAY, THE TRUTH, AND THE LIFE

Key Verse: *John 14:1-6 (ESV)*

"Let not your hearts be troubled. Believe in God; believe also in me… I go to prepare a place for you… I am the way, and the truth, and the life. No one comes to the Father except through me."

Day 1

Mission Insight

These words were spoken by Jesus just before His crucifixion, as He comforted His disciples during their growing fear and confusion. Anyone who has served knows what it feels like to face an uncertain future; change, loss, transitions, even mortality. Jesus speaks directly to the troubled heart. He does not deny the presence of fear, but He offers Himself as the answer, to trust Him. Jesus is not one way among many; He IS the way. And He has prepared a place, a future, and a hope for all who follow Him.

Personal Inspection

What do you see when you look at the place Jesus has made for you?

Prayer

Jesus, when my heart is troubled, help me turn to You. Remind me that You are the way; you have already laid out the path and You have already made a place for me.

Day 2

Mission Insight

"Let not your hearts be troubled..." These words do not discount anxiety they challenge it with trust. When you signed up you knew you would be navigating unknowns in your future; job changes, health concerns, grief, what war and when. Yet you can take comfort your heart isn't alone, Christ walks with you, do not let this world trouble you, believe in Him more than the world's troubles.

Personal Inspection

What is troubling your heart today and what would it look like to believe Jesus right there?

Prayer

Lord, You know what is weighing on me. Teach me to trust You, even when I do not understand.

Day 3

Mission Insight

"I go to prepare a place for you..." Jesus is not just offering help now He's securing your future. The military requires clear intent and guidance in the execution of its mission; the end state is made clear when Jesus tell us a place at the finish line awaits; your destination is handled, your place is ready. You are an expected resident returning home, the light is quite literally on for you.

Personal Inspection

How does knowing Jesus is preparing a place for you affect how you live today?

Prayer

Jesus, thank You for the promise of a home that's permanent and perfect. Help me live with eternity in view.

Day 4

Mission Insight

"I am the way…" Not a way, "the way". When we serve, we are given right and left limits that are to clarify what we are to do and what the outcome should be, all this is done for clarity of mission yet there is always ambiguity of sorts. Jesus in his time on Earth was more specific, He gave us our mission and "the way", the only way, and that way is the path to peace, purpose, and everlasting life, and it begins and ends with Christ.

Personal Inspection

Are you walking in His way or still lost trying to find your own way?

Prayer

Lord, guide my steps. Show me again that You are the way even when I wander bring me back to where I need to be, and that is with You.

Day 5

Mission Insight

"I am the truth…" In a world of blurred lines, Jesus offers clarity. When used to black-and-white orders we can still wrestle with moral gray areas during or after service, especially when dealing with the civilian side of life. What is right anymore may not always seem clear or as well-known as before. However when it comes to Jesus, He is the only way, with Jesus there is no confusion, live for and through him and you don't have to worry about the rest.

Personal Inspection
What false beliefs or voices do you need to replace with the truth of Jesus?

Prayer
God, I want to be anchored in truth. Let Your voice drown out the noise and let your Truth rise above all else.

Day 6

Mission Insight
"I am the life…" Many former service members struggle with identity and purpose after service, if you're not there yet you will be one day. Jesus does not only offer eternal life after this one, He offers abundant life now, whenever and wherever you're at. He is life itself, He's not just about getting by or surviving, but renewal, new life; live for Him in all you do, approach life in faith and the purpose will deliver itself.

Personal Inspection
What would it look like to experience Christ as your life, not just your belief?

Prayer
Jesus, breathe life into the places I have gone numb and make me new, born again; let me live in You, not just talk about You.

Day 7 After-Action Reflection

This week reminded us that Jesus is not simply a guide He is the destination, the map, and the journey. My friend, you don't need to have come up with every answer you just need to follow the One who is the answer. When your heart is troubled, you have a Savior who has prepared a place for you and walks beside you. You are not lost you are being led.

Auxiliary Scriptures

- *Psalm 23:1–4* "He leads me beside still waters… even though I walk through the valley…"
- *Revelation 21:3–4* "He will wipe every tear from their eyes…"

Prayer

Jesus, You are my way. You are my truth. You are my life. In You, I have peace, hope, love, and I am never alone or without a home.

Field Note

St. Stephen, one of the first deacons and the first Christian martyr, lived and died trusting in the way, truth, and life of Christ. In Acts 6:7, Stephen served the poor, boldly preached the gospel, and stood firm under false accusation saying to his accusers "Behold, I see the heavens opened and the Son of Man standing at the right hand of God." (Acts 7:56) Stephen's heart was not troubled, even in death while actively being stoned, he trusted the One who had prepared a place for him. (Crossway Bibles 2016) His life reflects John 14:1–6: unwavering belief in Jesus as the only way, the deepest truth, and eternal life.

WEEK 51 † GREATEST COMMANDMENT

Key Verse: *Mark 12:28-34 (ESV)*

"You shall love the Lord your God with all your heart… and your neighbor as yourself."

Day 1

Mission Insight

When asked which commandment mattered most, Jesus did not hesitate. Loving God and your neighbor is the core of it all. In speak we may best understand, this verse reframes the mission along two consecutive lines of communication. Loving God with heart, soul, mind, and body in full devotion. It involves emotion, thought, endurance, and will. And loving others? That is where faith becomes visible. In service, camaraderie often builds strong bonds, but Jesus calls us to extend that love beyond only our circle. This isn't just a religion it's the lifestyle of a kingdom citizen who loves God deeply, and let that love flow outward to all.

Personal Inspection

When you realize these two commandments cover all of the commandments, does it represent how you live your life?

Prayer
Lord, teach me how to love You with all I am. And help me love others like You have loved me, sacrificially, sincerely, and daily.

Day 2

Mission Insight
"Love the Lord your God with all…" You understand total commitment, you've proven that; giving all of yourself in upholding an oath, executing a mission, and fulfilling your service obligation. Jesus says our love for God should be just as complete, loving God in whole and fulfilled by all of who we are.

Personal Inspection
What part of your heart, soul, mind, or strength have you withheld from God?

Prayer
God, I give You not just pieces of me, but all of me. Teach me to love You with every part of who I am.

Day 3

Mission Insight
"Love your neighbor as yourself…" Do you know what it means to look out for each other, of course you do you've proven that by what you've already done. Jesus challenges us to extend that care not just to fellow comrades but to everyone we encounter. God's love is not only for a select few it is offered to all; He looks to us to follow His example and make our love for our fellow man open to all. Let it be up to them to receive it, and not that they never got a chance because it was never offered.

Personal Inspection
Who is your "neighbor" right now, and how can you serve them this week?

Prayer
Jesus, expand my definition of neighbor. Show me who needs love today, and help me to not only recognize that need but let me respond.

Day 4

Mission Insight
Loving God and loving others isn't optional. Jesus links them together, there is no doing one and not the other as believers of Jesus. You cannot just fill up the tank and forget to put air in the tires, it is the whole of the sum that makes this commandment from Jesus so important. What good is it to you to love God yet hate your neighbor, but yet this still happens far too often.

Personal Inspection
Is your love for God showing up in how you treat others? Where might that love be missing?

Prayer
Lord, let my love for You spill over into every relationship. Help me be known as one who loves all as you love all of your children.

Day 5

Mission Insight
"With all your mind..." Loving God isn't just about passion, or physically showing up, it includes your thoughts, convictions, and

worldview. While serving we had to maintain ourselves physically, challenge ourselves mentally, and be continuous learners. This same approach can apply to our faith, and a key component is giving our mind to Christ through spiritual reflection, reading Scripture, study, and intentional worship.

Personal Inspection

How are you engaging your mind in your love for God not just physically going through the motions?

Prayer

God, shape my thinking today, and help me seek and understand your truth with my whole mind.

Day 6

Mission Insight

"You are not far from the kingdom of God." That is what Jesus said to the man who understood the importance of love and what Jesus had said. Some of us may wonder how close we are to God; Jesus gives the answer, it begins with loving God and your neighbor, and then you are extremely close to the Kingdom of God. So rather than wonder do this, and then you know you're close.

Personal Inspection

What simple act of love can draw you closer to the heart of God today?

Prayer

Jesus, keep me close to Your kingdom not just in theory, but in how I live and how I love.

Day 7 After-Action Reflection

This week brought us back to basics; you have been trained to carry and withstand heavy burdens but the most vital thing we must learn in life is to love. Love God with everything, that means in all parts of your life. Love others like you want to be loved and as Jesus loved us. Loving God or others does not make you less of a warrior, it's what says matters most. If you get this right, everything else begins to fall into place.

Auxiliary Scriptures

- *1 John 4:19–21* "We love because he first loved us..."
- *Romans 13:10* "Love does no wrong to a neighbor; therefore love is the fulfilling of the law."

Prayer

Father, don't let me overlook the obvious. Help me love You with all I am, and love others with the same grace You've shown me.

Field Note

Colonel Robert Gould Shaw, commander of the 54th Massachusetts Volunteer Infantry, the first African American regiment organized during the Civil War. Shaw who was white volunteered to lead the 54th, fully aware of the risks and prejudice both he and his men would face. He led with humility and respected those under his command. Shaw refused his pay until his men could be compensated equally, and he ultimately died leading them in a courageous but deadly assault on Fort Wagner in 1863. He was buried with his soldiers, a gesture meant to disgrace him by Confederate forces, but which became a lasting symbol of solidarity. (Hardy 2000) Shaw's life was a great illustration of Mark 12:28–34 showing what it means to love God with all your being and love your neighbor as yourself even at great personal cost.

WEEK 52 † BORN AGAIN

Key Verse: *John 3:5-7 (ESV)*

"Truly I say to you, unless one is born of water and the Spirit, he cannot enter the kingdom of God... That which is born of the flesh is flesh, and that which is born of the Spirit is spirit... You must be born again."

Day 1

Mission Insight

I purposefully saved this verse for last for the emphasis on how we are made new. Jesus spoke these words to Nicodemus, a respected religious leader who thought he had it all figured out. But Jesus challenged him and us to see faith not as improvement, but as rebirth. Veterans may relate to the idea of reinvention: leaving one life behind and stepping into a new one changing from one mission or task to the next. But spiritual rebirth goes deeper. It is not about upgrading who we are it is about receiving a whole new identity through the Holy Spirit. Being "born again" is not a label it is a complete and total transformation. It is the foundation of your citizenship in God's kingdom and example set by the lives of the apostles.

Personal Inspection

What does being born of the spirit mean to you, what defines you more, your flesh or your spirit?

Prayer
Lord Jesus, thank You for making me new. Help me live today in light of who I am in You and the spirit not just who I was in the flesh.

Day 2

Mission Insight
"Born of water and the Spirit..." Water represents cleansing; the Spirit brings life. You may understand physical training and ritual but Jesus is talking about a heart change that only God can do, a change that happens before the symbolism of baptism takes place. This is not boot camp or a specialty school, it's surrender of your old life turning it in for a new one.

Personal Inspection
Have you invited God to remake you not just fix you?

Prayer
God, wash me clean. Fill me with Your Spirit. Make me new from the inside out.

Day 3

Mission Insight
"You must be born again." This is a requirement, not a suggestion. Men and women that were in the service are used to following mission critical orders, you should see this as one; you must be spiritually reborn, there is no substitute for entering God's kingdom. And how glorious it is after all the miles under those feet, the wear and tear of this world, you can still be made new!

Personal Inspection
Have you experienced that new birth and if so, how has your life changed?

Prayer
Lord, thank You for giving me new life. Help me walk in it fully and let go of my past.

Day 4

Mission Insight
Jesus' words to Nicodemus shattered his assumptions. Sometimes, like veterans moving into or navigating the civilian world, or assuming a new rank and position, our former identity must die for a new one to rise. Being born again may feel disorienting, however over time it leads to the deepest clarity and purpose.

Personal Inspection
What part of your old life is God calling you to release so He can give you something new?

Prayer
Jesus, give me courage to let go of what no longer defines me and embrace who I am in You.

Day 5

Mission Insight
The Spirit gives birth to spirit. Your rebirth in Christ is much like first entering the military it gives you a new identity, new family, and new purpose. This is like that, except instead of serving your country and handing them a blank check with your life you are

serving God and letting him spend the investment He has made in your life. You are not who you were, you are who He says you are, and you are in His image.

Personal Inspection

What truth about your new identity in Christ do you need to remind yourself of today?

Prayer

Holy Spirit, remind me I am a child of God no longer bound to the past but born into purpose.

Day 6

Mission Insight

"Do not marvel…" Jesus knew Nicodemus would struggle with this idea many of us have. In rank structured professions we may be used to earning status or respect, much like Nicodemus had a lofty status and believed his worthiness was more before God because of it. But rebirth cannot be earned by lofty titles or accomplishments, it is a gift. All you can do is receive it and live from it.

Personal Inspection

Are you still trying to earn what God has already given you?

Prayer

Father, I receive the gift of new life. Teach me to live like it is truly mine and that I am Yours.

Day 7 After-Action Reflection

This week brought us back to the beginning, your spiritual birth. Brothers and Sisters, you have experienced changes in title, role, or uniform but this change is once and lasts forever. When you're born of the Spirit, everything else becomes secondary. You are a new creation, not defined by your past and not disqualified by your failures. You have been made new and you are now part of something permanent and indestructible.

Auxiliary Scriptures

- *2 Corinthians 5:17* "If anyone is in Christ, he is a new creation..."
- *Titus 3:5* "He saved us... by the washing of regeneration and renewal of the Holy Spirit."

Prayer

Jesus, thank You for giving me a new start not once, but every day. Help me live like someone who has been made new because I am.

Field Note

Constantine the Great, Roman Emperor from A.D. 306 to 337, is known for his role in the Christianization of the Roman Empire. While raised in a culture steeped in paganism and imperial cult worship, Constantine experienced a pivotal shift before the Battle of the Milvian Bridge in A.D. 312. According to Eusebius, Constantine saw a vision of a cross with the words "By this conquer." He ordered his troops to mark their shields with the Christian symbol and won the battle. Following this, Constantine increasingly aligned himself with Christian faith, issuing the Edict of Milan in A.D. 313, which granted religious freedom and ended persecution of Christians. He supported the Church and was finally baptized shortly before his death. (Super 2012) Constantine's journey, though gradual, reflected the essence of John 3:5–7: a man shaped by empire and power who was ultimately born again by water and Spirit.

ABOUT THE AUTHOR

Lieutenant Colonel Curt W. Kolvet grew up in Minden, Nevada, a small valley town near Lake Tahoe in the Sierra Nevada Mountains. Raised alongside an older sister and younger brother, he spent his early years playing sports, riding horses, and serving as an altar boy at his local Catholic church. After moving to Reno at age twelve, he attended Bishop Manogue Catholic High School, graduating in 1997. There, he served as a captain on the football, baseball, and debate teams, earning All-State honors as a quarterback and league MVP in baseball. At sixteen, he was selected to Team USA for the Goodwill Baseball Series and traveled to Beijing, China to compete internationally.

In May 2001, Curt graduated from the University of Nevada with a Bachelor of Arts in Criminal Justice and a minor in Philosophy, while simultaneously receiving his commission as a Second Lieutenant in the U.S. Army Ordnance Corps. Following his initial training at Aberdeen Proving Ground, Maryland, he reported to his first duty station in Würzburg, Germany.

From 2004 to 2005, Curt deployed to Tikrit, Iraq with the 1st Infantry Division in support of Operation Iraqi Freedom II, where he was promoted to Captain. During this deployment, he served in multiple logistics leadership roles and commanded more than twenty Combat Logistics Patrol missions. He was awarded the Combat Action Badge following an improvised explosive device attack on his vehicle. Throughout the deployment, he experienced frequent rocket and mortar attacks, an anti-vehicle mine incident, and multiple IED events. While deployed, Curt's son Thomas was born; he first met him at five weeks old during mid-tour leave.

After completing his active-duty obligation, Curt returned to Reno and began a civilian career with Dell Computers, working in operations and project management at the company's West Coast Fulfillment Center. During this period, he and his family welcomed their daughter, Cora. After five years in the private sector, Curt felt called to return to the military and reentered full-time service as an Active-Duty Guardsman with the Nevada Army National Guard.

In 2012, as a Company Commander, Curt led the 593rd Transportation Company on a standalone deployment to Kabul, Afghanistan in support of Operation Enduring Freedom 12–13. His unit conducted security force operations, convoy escorts, and quick reaction force missions throughout the RC-Capital region, utilizing MRAPs and other up-armored vehicles. During the deployment, his company faced car bomb attacks, rocket fire, and civil unrest.

Following his return, Curt was promoted to Major and later to Lieutenant Colonel in 2020. Over the course of his career, he served 5 years overseas (Iraq, Kuwait, Afghanistan, Kyrgyzstan, Germany, Romania, Hawaii, & Fiji) and more than 80 months in command, including two tours as Battalion Commander of the 757th Combat Sustainment Support Battalion. His additional assignments included Battalion Executive Officer, Brigade Operations Officer, State Training Officer, Adjunct Professor of Military Science at the University of Nevada, Director of Logistics, Deputy Director of Human Resources and Manpower, and Joint Plans Director. From 2021 to 2023, he was awarded the Armed Forces Service Medal for his contributions to the COVID-19 response.

Curt is a graduate of the Command and General Staff Officer Course at Fort Leavenworth, Kansas, and earned a Master of Science in Human Relations and Business from Amberton University, a private Christian university, in 2016.

He plans to retire from military service in 2026, grateful for the opportunity to serve alongside Soldiers, families, and allied partners from multiple nations. Throughout every season of his life, Curt's faith has remained constant. Raised in the Catholic Church, he later embraced a non-denominational Christian walk and has been part of the same church community in Reno since 2011. Following retirement, he looks forward to continued service through study, writing, evangelism, and volunteer work.

Curt's military awards and decorations include the Bronze Star Medal, Meritorious Service Medal (four awards), Army Commendation Medal (four awards), Army Achievement Medal, Iraq Campaign Medal, Afghanistan Campaign Medal, Armed Forces Service Medal, NATO ISAF Medal, Combat Action Badge, German Armed Forces Military Proficiency Badge (Gold), and multiple additional service and unit awards.

BIBLIOGRAPHY

"Abraham Lincoln and the Bible – Abraham Lincoln's Classroom." 2025. Abrahamlincolnsclassroom.org. 2025. https://www.abrahamlincolnsclassroom.org/abraham-lincoln-in-depth/abraham-lincoln-and-the-bible/index.html.

"Army Surgeon General Meets with Double-Arm Transplant Recipient Sgt. Brendan Marrocco." 2013. Www.army.mil. February 13, 2013. https://www.army.mil/article/96366/army_surgeon_general_meets_with_double_arm_transplant_recipient_sgt_brendan_marrocco.

"The Bravery of Army Nurse Annie G. Fox at Pearl Harbor." n.d. National Women's History Museum. https://www.womenshistory.org/articles/bravery-army-nurse-annie-g-fox-pearl-harbor.

Broder, John M. 1991. "Schwarzkopf's War Plan Based on Deception." Los Angeles Times. Los Angeles Times. February 28, 1991. https://www.latimes.com/archives/la-xpm-1991-02-28-mn-2834-story.html.

"Cana Academy — Ernest Gordon: Building Heaven in the Midst of POW Hell." n.d. Cana Academy. https://www.canaacademy.org/blog/ernest-gordon-building-heaven-in-the-midst-of-pow-hell.

"Catholic Military Chaplain Who Witnessed 9/11 Sees Goodness in National Unity 10 Years Later - Archdiocese for the Military, USA." 2011. Archdiocese for the Military, USA. September 9, 2011.

https://www.milarch.org/catholic-military-chaplain-who-witnessed-911-sees-goodness-in-national-unity-10-years-later/.

Ciara Berry. 2016. "Alfred 'the Great' (R. 871-899)." The Royal Family. March 11, 2016. https://www.royal.uk/alfred-great-r-871-899.

"The Creation of 'Amazing Grace' | Articles and Essays | Amazing Grace | Digital Collections | Library of Congress." 2015. The Library of Congress. 2015. https://www.loc.gov/collections/amazing-grace/articles-and-essays/creation-of-amazing-grace.

Crossway Bibles. 2016. *ESV: Study Bible: English Standard Version.* Wheaton, Ill.: Crossway Bibles.

"Desmond Thomas Doss: World War II: U.S. Army: Medal of Honor Recipient." Congressional Medal of Honor Society. Accessed July 8, 2025. https://www.cmohs.org/recipients/desmond-t-doss.

"FDR's Faith." 2023. The Christian Century. 2023. https://www.christiancentury.org/books/fdr-s-faith.

Flick, Dr Stephen. 2022. "Alvin York, Christian Hero." Christian Heritage Fellowship, Inc. November 13, 2022. https://christianheritagefellowship.com/alvin-york-christian-hero/.

Fr. Stavros Akrotirianakis. 2024. "Out of the Depths | from Sinner to Saint—St. Longinus." Orthodox Christian Network. May 3, 2024. https://myocn.net/out-of-the-depths-from-sinner-to-saint-st-longinus.

"Gail Halvorsen | American Experience | PBS." n.d. Www.pbs.org. https://www.pbs.org/wgbh/americanexperience/features/airlift-gail-halvorsen/.

Galloway, Noah. 2019. "Noah Galloway." Noah Galloway. 2019. https://www.noahgalloway.com.

"George Muller Biography." 2024. GeorgeMuller.org. 2024. https://www.georgemuller.org/devotional/category/biography.

Grossman on Truth. 2024. "Grossman on Truth." Grossman on Truth. July 15, 2024. https://grossmanontruth.com.

Hardy, James D. 2000. "Duty First: Robert Gould Shaw in His Own Words and His Biographer's." *Civil War Book Review* 2 (1). https://doi.org/10.31390/cwbr.2.1.12.

Healy, Caitlin. n.d. "National Museum of the United States Army." Www.thenmusa.org. https://www.thenmusa.org/biographies/george-c-marshall/.

Herrick, Carolyn. 2012. Review of Meeting Bataan Survivors Taught Me about History, God, and Service. 49th Wing Public Affairs. March 26, 2012. https://www.holloman.af.mil/News/Commentaries/Display/Article/318953/meeting-bataan-survivors-taught-me-about-history-god-and-service/.

Houston, Sam. 2022. "Houston's Spiritual Journey - Today@Sam - Sam Houston State University." SHSU. 2022. https://www.shsu.edu/today@sam/samhouston/SamSp.html.

Jackson, Josh, and Josh Jackson. 2019. "Indivisible, the Story of Darren and Heather Turner | Episode 28 - Officers' Christian Fellowship." Officers' Christian Fellowship. January 28, 2019. https://www.ocfusa.org/2019/01/indivisible-turner-episode-28/.

Joyce. 2020. "Great Leaders Don't Pass the Buck." *Forbes*, September 26, 2020. https://www.forbes.com/sites/joyceearussell/2020/09/26/great-leaders-dont-pass-the-buck.

Leigh. 2013. "The Testimony of Eddie Rickenbacker." Fatherscall.com. March 22, 2013. https://fatherscall.com/2013/03/22/the-testimony-of-eddie-rickenbacker/.

"Lt. Col. Charles Kettles | Medal of Honor Recipient | U.S. Army." 2016. Army.mil. 2016. https://www.army.mil/medalofhonor/kettles/.

"MAJ Richard D. Winters." n.d. Militaryhallofhonor.com. https://militaryhallofhonor.com/honoree-record.php?id=3239.

"Medal of Honor Monday: Army Staff Sgt. Clint Romesha." 2025. U.S. Department of Defense. 2025. https://www.defense.gov/News/Feature-Stories/Story/Article/3932875/medal-of-honor-monday-army-staff-sgt-clint-romesha/.

Mockenhaupt, Brian. 2009. "What I've Learned: Bryan Anderson." Esquire. November 11, 2009. https://www.esquire.com/news-politics/interviews/a2320/esq0107bryananderson/.

National Archives. 2019. "Quotes | Eisenhower Presidential Library." Eisenhowerlibrary.gov. 2019. https://www.eisenhowerlibrary.gov/eisenhowers/quotes.

National Museum of African American History & Culture. n.d. "Remembering the Harlem Hellfighters." National Museum of African American History and Culture. https://nmaahc.si.edu/explore/stories/remembering-harlem-hellfighters.

"National Museum of the United States Army." n.d. Www.thenmusa.org. https://www.thenmusa.org/biographies/sharon-a-lane/.

National Park Service. 2016. "General von Steuben - Valley Forge National Historical Park (U.S. National Park Service)." Nps.gov. 2016. https://www.nps.gov/vafo/learn/historyculture/vonsteuben.htm.

National Park Service. 2017. "Harriet Tubman and the Underground Railroad (U.S. National Park Service)." Nps.gov. March 11, 2017. https://www.nps.gov/articles/harriet-tubman-and-the-underground-railroad.htm.

"Nelson Mandela - Biography." 2019. Mandela.gov.za. 2019. http://www.mandela.gov.za/biography/index.html.

The New York Times. 1955. "With Courage Born of Faith; GORDON of KHARTOUM. The Life of Gen. Charles George Gordon. By Lord Elton. Illustrated. 376 Pp. New York: Alfred A. Knopf. $6.," January 16, 1955. https://www.nytimes.com/1955/01/16/archives/with-courage-born-of-faith-gordon-of-khartoum-the-life-of-gen.html.

News article: La Times, Schwarzkopf's War Plan Based on Deception, by John M. Broder 2/28/1991 https://www.latimes.com/archives/la-xpm-1991-02-28-mn-2834-story.html

Review of *Captain Gary M. Rose*. 2018. Military Review the Professional Journal of the U.S. Army. April 2018. https://www.armyupress.army.mil/Journals/Military-Review/English-Edition-Archives/March-April-2018/MoH/.

Review of *COMMAND SGT. MAJ. BENNIE G. ADKINS*. n.d. DISTINGUISHED MEMBER of the SPECIAL FORCES REGIMENT. U.S. Army John F. Kennedy Special Warfare Center and School. 2010. https://www.swcs.mil/Portals/111/sf_adkins.pdf.

"Sergeant First Class Alwyn C. Cashe." n.d. Www.army.mil. https://www.army.mil/medalofhonor/cashe/.

Selanders, Louise. 2019. "Florence Nightingale - Homecoming and Legacy." In *Encyclopædia Britannica.* https://www.britannica.com/biography/Florence-Nightingale/Homecoming-and-legacy.

Shelton, Jenni. n.d. "The Spiritual Mandela: Faith and Religion in the Life of Nelson the Spiritual Mandela: Faith and Religion in the Life of Nelson Mandela Mandela." *The Journal of Traditions & Beliefs the Journal of Traditions & Beliefs* 6 (10). https://engagedscholarship.csuohio.edu/cgi/viewcontent.cgi?article=1099&context=jtb.

Smith, Gary Scott. 2024. "D-Day and the Faith of Dwight Eisenhower." The Institute for Faith and Freedom. June 3, 2024. https://www.faithandfreedom.com/d-day-and-the-faith-of-dwight-eisenhower/.

"St. Joan of Arc - FaithND." 2024. FaithND. September 19, 2024. https://faith.nd.edu/saint/st-joan-of-arc/.

"The Stockdale Paradox – Vibrant Faith." 2022. Vibrantfaith.org. March 4, 2022. https://vibrantfaith.org/the-stockdale-paradox/.

Super. 2012. "The Battle of Milvian Bridge and the History of the Book." Library News. November 1, 2012. https://library.missouri.edu/news/special-collections/the-battle-of-milvian-bridge-and-the-history-of-the-book.

Ten Boom, Corrie, Elizabeth Sherrill, John L. Sherrill, and Joni Earekson Tada. 2015. *The Hiding Place.* [New York]: Baker Publishing Group.

Transportation Corps, Army.mil. 2023. https://transportation.army.mil/history/studies/red_ball_express.html.

United States Holocaust Memorial Museum, Washington, DC. 2009. "Dietrich Bonhoeffer." Ushmm.org. 2009. https://encyclopedia.ushmm.org/content/en/article/dietrich-bonhoeffer.

"US Army Chaplain, Korean War POW and Future Saint? Father Emil Kapaun Now 'Venerable' - Catholic Standard." 2025. Catholic Standard. 2025. https://www.cathstan.org/faith/us-army-chaplain-korean-war-pow-and-future-saint-father-emil-kapaun-now-venerable.

Veterans Airlift. 2007. "Meet Scott Smiley - Veterans Airlift Command." Veterans Airlift Command - Give Our Combat Injured the Wings They Need. July 24, 2007. https://veteransairlift.org/news/2007/07/meet-scott-smiley/.

Vatican. n.d. "Mother Teresa of Calcutta (1910-1997), Biography." Www.vatican.va. https://www.vatican.va/news_services/liturgy/saints/ns_lit_doc_20031019_madre-teresa_en.html.

White, Ronald C. 2024. *On Great Fields*. Random House.

Made in the USA
Coppell, TX
21 June 2026

82754017R00177